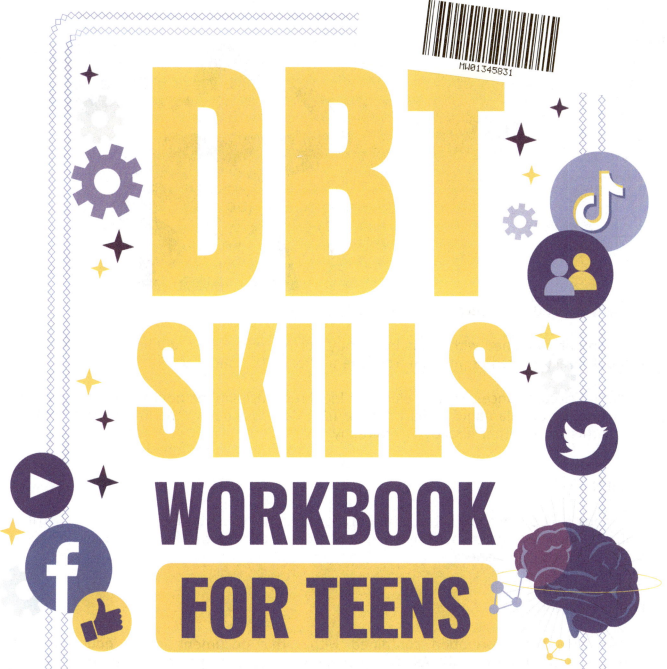

© Copyright 2024 Isabella Finn - All rights reserved

The content contained within this book may not be reproduced, duplicated or transmitted without direct written permission from the author or the publisher.

Under no circumstances will any blame or legal responsibility be held against the publisher, or author, for any damages, reparation, or monetary loss due to the information contained within this book, either directly or indirectly.

Legal Notice:

This book is copyright protected. It is only for personal use. You cannot amend, distribute, sell, use, quote or paraphrase any part, or the content within this book, without the consent of the author or publisher.

Disclaimer Notice:

Please note the information contained within this document is for educational and entertainment purposes only. All effort has been executed to present accurate, up to date, reliable, complete information. No warranties of any kind are declared or implied. Readers acknowledge that the author is not engaged in the rendering of legal, financial, medical or professional advice. The content within this book has been derived from various sources. Please consult a licensed professional before attempting any techniques outlined in this book.

By reading this document, the reader agrees that under no circumstances is the author responsible for any losses, direct or indirect, that are incurred as a result of the use of the information contained within this document, including, but not limited to, errors, omissions, or inaccuracies.

Get Your 4 Complimentary E-books!

Scan the QR code with the camera on your phone to get full access or go to https://www.isabellafinn.com/dbtbonus

Questions? Feel free to email me at isabella@isabellafinn.com

ISABELLA FINN

To Learn More Go to https://isabellafinn.com or Scan the QR code below:

Table of Contents

Introduction — 6

Chapter 1: Understanding DBT and Its Skills — 9
- Understanding Dialectical Behavior Therapy (DBT) — 9
- Benefits of DBT for Teens — 10
- The Science Behind DBT's Effectiveness — 11
- Misconceptions about DBT — 12
- The Role of Parents as Allies and Partners — 14

Chapter 2: Mindfulness for DBT — 16
- What is Mindfulness? — 16
- Benefits of a Mindful Lifestyle — 17
- Mindfulness from a DBT Perspective — 19
- Mindfulness Exercises — 21

Chapter 3: Emotion Regulation — 24
- Understanding Your Emotions — 24
  - Identifying Your Emotions — 26
  - Challenging Negative Thought Patterns — 27
  - Building Emotional Resilience — 29
  - Emotion Regulation Exercises — 31

Chapter 4: Distress Tolerance — 37
- Understanding Distress and Its Impact — 37
  - How to Cope with Distress — 40
  - Distress Tolerance Exercises — 44

Chapter 5: Interpersonal Effectiveness — 49
- Understanding Interpersonal Effectiveness — 49
- Effective Communication Skills and Assertiveness — 50
- Creating Boundaries and Managing Conflicts — 57
- Conflict Resolution Using DBT Principles — 60
- Interpersonal Effectiveness Exercises — 61

Chapter 6: Coping with Stressors — 65
Understanding Your Stress Triggers — 66
    Organizing Your Life to Minimize Stress — 69
    Exercises to Cope with Stressors — 71

Chapter 7: Social Media and Mental Health — 73
    Benefits of Social Media — 73
    Drawbacks of Social Media for Teens — 75
    Digital Detox — 77
    Digital Detox Exercises — 80

Chapter 8: Self-Care and Self-Compassion — 90
    Understanding Self-Care and Self-Compassion — 90
    The Need for Self-Care and Self-Compassion — 91
    Nurturing Self-Care — 93
    Self-Compassion in Tough Times — 94
    Exercises — 95

Conclusion — 98

References — 99

Introduction

> *"You don't have to control your thoughts. You just have to stop letting them control you."*
>
> - Dan Millman, Author and Personal Development Lecturer

You're sitting at your desk, surrounded by notes, textbooks, and the crippling thoughts of the deadline of an assignment you've been putting off. Now, your mind feels chaotic, with countless thoughts moving faster than you can catch them. Sound familiar?

We've all had moments when we're faced with so many pressures from home, school, and social drama that it feels like we're riding a rollercoaster with no seatbelt to protect us from falling.

But regardless of how overwhelming and chaotic the teenage years may seem, know that you have the power to enjoy life. In fact, you're about to embark on an exciting adventure filled with knowledge to gracefully navigate life's twists and turns.

Surviving your teenage years may seem hard. You might struggle with the day-to-day activities and feel unworthy, ill-prepared, or confused. The world may seem like a scary place where you'll never belong. These internal emotions and unrest can negatively impact your perspective and approach to life.

You may often find yourself in a bad mood. You may feel overwhelmed by responsibilities and the expectations people have of you. There's a lot of pressure to perform well at school and in sports, build and maintain meaningful relationships, and discover who you are. Soon enough, negative thoughts might creep into your mind: *I'm not good enough.*

When will I get my life together? Everyone has their life figured out except me!

As untruthful as these thoughts are, you may think them so often that you start to believe them. Could it be you're the only teenager who doesn't have their life together? The answer is a resounding NO! You'd be shocked at how many teenagers have the same experience as you.

Maybe you're ashamed of these thoughts and have been acting confident and happy around your friends so they won't judge you negatively. But have you ever tried talking about your feelings with them? Have you ever asked them if they deal with similar negative thoughts? Have you ever tried to bring up the idea of anxiety and how it affects you? These questions may sound simple, but many teens avoid asking them for fear of being judged or being seen as stupid or uncool.

I'd like to challenge you to ask your friends these questions next time you see them. Believe me, you will hear interesting answers. Some of your friends will tell you they struggle with their mood, they are often stressed, have eating disorders, thoughts about self-harm, and low self-worth. Many will also admit that they feel like they can't deal with these emotions.

The point is that you are not alone. Research indicates that teenage anxiety has been on the rise, increasing by up to 20% between 2007 and 2012 (Nutt E. A., 2018). What's more, Gen Z is reportedly more stressed than any previous generation. If this trend continues, we can assume Gen Alpha, the youngest generation, feels the same. The big question now is, why? Why are younger generations more troubled? There are many reasons, but let's talk about three of the most compelling ones.

First is social media. The number of likes, followers, and shares has a huge impact on how many teenagers perceive themselves. Often, teens will compare themselves unfavorably to others on social media, thinking that everyone else has a better life than them.

Second, many people are living through tough and changing economic times. The future seems uncertain, even for the most developed economies in the world. People are losing their jobs and being laid off. This can instill fear among teenagers about what the future holds for them.

As if that isn't enough, attending college has become the norm these days, so academic expectations have continued to increase. Everyone expects you to study hard, excel in all your classes, get into a good college, and land a good job so you can live a "good" life. If you don't get into college, many consider you doomed to a life of mediocrity. Society today expects you to be better and do better.

It's not surprising, then, that so many teens struggle with mental health issues. You've probably met a teen who doesn't know how to manage triggers or navigate stressful situations. Maybe some of your friends find it hard to communicate their feelings without breaking down or, worse, becoming aggressive. Some of them don't set firm boundaries or stand by them. It's a real struggle.

But is this how it's supposed to be? Should you and your friends accept that this is how it is? Should you all go through your teenage years anxious, stressed, and full of negative thoughts and emotions? Of course not. I've always believed that the secret to living a happy, healthy life is learning to deal with our struggles, embracing them, and going through life as our authentic selves. Sadly, it's during our challenging adolescent years that we often lose ourselves while trying to get a handle on our physical and emotional challenges.

Ever heard the phrase, *"Tough times don't last?"* Well, you're going to learn those words are true, because you're about to gain access to Dialectical Behavior Therapy (DBT). DBT is a talk therapy that introduces you to a treasure trove of skills, techniques, and strategies to help you thrive in the face of life's challenges. It's like having a secret superhero toolkit filled with everything you need to conquer self-doubt, stress, and anxiety.

I have two incredible teenagers, and I can tell you for a fact that I've seen it all. I've held their hands and been a pillar of support while they had to deal with many emotional troubles and self-doubt. I have written this book in the hope that it will help you and other teenagers by teaching you DBT skills and strategies, so we can lower the staggering mental health statistics for teens that are being reported today.

> But this isn't just a book. This is a workbook designed to teach you how to find a balance between accepting who you are and changing the things you don't like about yourself. This is the foundational element of DBT. The main goals of this book are to teach you how to improve your mental health using mindfulness practices, show you how to navigate the wild, scary seas of overwhelming emotions using emotion regulation techniques, teach you how to become the master of your thoughts so you can rein in the stressful and anxious ones, and train you to overcome your negative thoughts and kick them out of your life once and for all.

Each chapter will teach you a new technique and sharpen your skills, so you have a better way of dealing with stress, negative thoughts, anxiety, and strong emotions.
This book is designed to exhaust both the theoretical and practical aspects of DBT. As you progress, you will find meaningful exercises that will teach you how to apply DBT skills practically.

Before we begin, it's important you know that you're capable of incredible growth and transformation, and that your journey is just beginning. Use this book as a guide, a friend, and a reminder that you have the power to create a life filled with joy, purpose, and resilience.

Let's get started!

Chapter 1
Understanding DBT and Its Skills

"Life' is a game we must all play, and it's filled with challenges we need to survive, especially as a teen. Dialectical Behavioral Therapy (DBT), is an effective tool that, when used, can help you easily manage all the heavy stones that life throws at you.

This chapter will discuss the skills you can gain from DBT and how to use them. What you'll learn here is practical knowledge that will help you navigate life. From struggling with anxiety to the stress of getting ready for school and every obstacle in between, DBT has got you covered and will improve your mental wellness.

Understanding Dialectical Behavior Therapy (DBT)

The term "dialectical" is derived from the idea of bringing two opposite concepts together to achieve results, rather than focusing on one. The goal of DBT is to use change and acceptance to bring relief, teach individuals to accept their experiences and change the negative behaviors that arise as a result of those experiences.

> DBT is a unique form of talk therapy (psychotherapy). Specifically, it's an evidence-based approach similar to the more commonly used Cognitive Behavioral Therapy (CBT). DBT is specifically designed for people who deal with intense emotions daily.
>
> DBT is rooted in science and philosophy and characterized by two important beliefs: *I am using what I have to do the best I can, and There are ways to do this better, so I have to try harder to learn them.*

The goal of this type of therapy is to help you understand your intense emotions, accept difficult emotions, learn the skills that will help you manage the intense emotions, and empower you to make positive life changes.

You're probably wondering, "But how can I do two things at the same time that seem like opposites?" How can you accept yourself, your behaviors, thoughts, and emotions and then also change those thoughts, behaviors, and emotions? Well, with DBT, this is possible.

DBT is based on CBT, which teaches us how to change our negative thought patterns and ultimately change the behaviors that often arise out of those negative thought patterns. DBT also teaches us how to change our negative thoughts and emotions and the behaviors associated with them, but it goes deeper than CBT, teaching us how to accept these negative emotions. There's more group work in DBT than in CBT. In DBT, you have to work hard to make positive changes in your life.

Another important concept that runs through DBT is that everything in life is connected. Change is the one constant we can all rely on. The idea is to identify a dysfunctional behavior, address it, and change the negative thought patterns that lead to the behavior. During use, you'll learn how to offset intense emotions with mindfulness practices and practical problem-solving skills.

Benefits of DBT for Teens

I'm sure you're trying to strike a balance with a lot of things, like school, friends, and other stresses of life. Well, you'll be glad to hear that's just where DBT comes in. It's the perfect tool to help you de-stress.

Here are some aspects of your life where DBT can be of great help:
- Self-harm
- Impulsivity
- Suicidal thoughts and attempts
- Mood and anxiety disorders
- Anger issues
- Eating disorders
- Attention-deficit hyperactivity disorder (ADHD)
- Personality disorders
- Substance abuse
- Low self-esteem
- Family and peer conflict

When you think of therapy, you might have the image of a stranger sitting across from you, bombarding you with tons of questions. DBT is different from the idea many of us have of standard therapy. It uses different techniques and skills during treatment. And though it isn't a magic wand that can fix the world's problems, it can work for you if applied properly and with consistency over time.

DBT will make your life less crazy if you're committed to making positive changes in yourself, are ready to put in the work, willing to focus on the now and the future rather than the past, and open to participating in group sessions with others.

This effective therapy includes group lectures, group discussions, and times when you're expected to practice what you're learning in groups. Group sessions usually take place at least once a week if you're working with a therapist, and it's important that you attend every session to get the most out of your therapy.

The Science Behind DBT's Effectiveness

DBT may sound like normal therapy, but it's actually a step beyond what we think of as standard therapy. It's more useful for teenagers because your brain at this age is still under construction. Whatever or whoever you want to be as an adult, either emotionally, physically, or even spiritually, the best time to lay the foundation is during your childhood and teenage years.

The part of the brain in charge of decision-making and impulse control is called the prefrontal cortex. It continues to develop in every human until the mid-20s. This is why when certain emotions set in, they can wear you out. But you know what? Apply DBT skills, and you'll find yourself easing your stress.

> Research has shown that DBT can improve how well we regulate our emotions. This can put you in more control of some emotional states that may make you act out of proportion to the circumstances. You don't need much; have your DBT skills at arm's length, and you're good to go. *Remember, you're the captain of your emotional ship, and how you cope with troubled seas lies solely with you.*

As you probably know, life is filled with emotional moments at different stages, and you have to learn how to face them and be bold enough to conquer them without losing yourself in the process. The more you use DBT, the better you'll become at improving and regulating your emotions.

> So where does mindfulness come into the picture? **Mindfulness is important in DBT because it's a good way of getting your brain to do some work and also helps with the regions of the brain that are involved in attention and emotion control.** Mindfulness helps boost those areas of the brain that help us focus. It's essential for DBT to work effectively.

Another core of DBT is neuroplasticity, which means how the brain changes and adapts. Every time you use DBT, you're taking your brain through a workout, which makes it happier and healthier. This makes room for stable emotions and better mental habits.

Many people think DBT is only for emotions, but it's also useful in other mental health fields. In fact, this therapy was initially intended to tackle Borderline Personality Disorder (BPD). But it has proven its usefulness in other fields, as well, like anxiety, depression, eating disorders, and even post-traumatic stress disorder (PTSD). It's a multi-relevant secret tool that you'll be happy to have at your fingertips.

An amazing bonus you'll find with DBT comes in your relationships with people around you. You'll unconsciously learn how to improve your communication skills and how to interact with family, friends, colleagues, and acquaintances.

Misconceptions about DBT

DBT has become quite popular in recent years as people learn more about its effectiveness and benefits. But its popularity hasn't been without downsides. Many have misconceptions about what DBT is and who it's meant to help.

Here are some of the most common myths surrounding DBT:

- **It's only effective for treating Borderline Personality Disorder (BPD).**

    DBT was originally designed to treat people with BPD. However, with more research on the subject, experts concluded that it's effective for a wide range of mental health disorders. Most mental health conditions are related to skill deficits like emotion regulation, distress tolerance, and mindfulness. Since DBT teaches these skills, it addresses many of these conditions from the root. For example, if someone is struggling with an eating disorder because they think they need to look a certain way to be worthy, DBT teaches them to identify those negative thought patterns, accept them as distorted, and change them into positive ones. Therefore, DBT isn't limited to BPD; it can be used to treat a wide range of mental health issues that result from distorted thought patterns.

- **It's too time-consuming.**

    DBT may require more time than traditional therapy, but it takes less time than other forms of treatment, like inpatient stays. What's more, the time you'll spend in treatment is significantly less than the time you spend being depressed and anxious, struggling with intense emotions, trying to repair relationships, and engaging in self-destructive coping mechanisms.

- **It's all about suicide prevention.**

    DBT isn't a suicide prevention program. Instead, I would describe it as a life-changing program. For many people who have chosen DBT, suicide may have seemed like the only way out of their suffering. But DBT taught them that their life is worth living and that they have the power to change things. DBT treatment does target suicide, suicidal thoughts, self-harm, and other self-destructive behaviors, but the goal is to help people build their lives back up and create something they can be proud of.

- **"DBT won't help me because nothing has helped me so far."**

    Many people turn to DBT after other types of therapy have failed. This could be because the other therapies didn't identify and effectively teach them the skills they need to deal with their challenges. In DBT, the idea is that insight alone isn't enough to sufficiently resolve one's emotional distress and self-destructive behaviors. DBT takes the insights and combines them with skills and structured therapy sessions to solve your problems.

- **"I'll have to do DBT for the rest of my life."**

    This couldn't be further from the truth. One of the main goals of DBT is recovery. A therapist will work with you, teaching you skills that will help you build a life that isn't dependent on therapy or treatments. The skills and techniques you learn in DBT are designed to help you cope independently with the problems that have been troubling you. Most DBT patients report full recovery, moving on to live happy, meaningful lives with significantly reduced suffering.

Develop the right mindset!

If you want to get the most out of your DBT journey, you'll have to develop the right mindset. As a teen, you are dealing with a unique set of emotions, heartaches, and challenges, so you have to figure out the right way to approach this.

First, understand what DBT is all about. That's exactly what this chapter covers — the basics. What is it? What therapy options are available? Think about what works best for you, but also listen to advice from experts on what can help you cope faster. Consider the skills you'll learn and how you will implement them in your life.

> DBT teaches people that they have more options than they think when dealing with emotional situations. **It's important to go into this with an open mind. Be willing to learn and embrace the journey of self-discovery.** Understand that without the right mindset, it will be impossible to figure out what skills will work for you or how to put them to use effectively.

You have to be willing to learn, do your homework, and show up every day. Build trust in the process you have started. Understand that commitment is a critical ingredient in your healing. You don't have to go all in at once, but you do need to show up. Set goals every other week and take small, consistent steps from the beginning to the end. No one is saying it will be easy. There are days you'll feel like you've had enough. That's when you need to hold tighter and refuse to give up.

Don't forget to celebrate your successes, no matter how small they seem. Even a single step in the right direction brings you closer to your goals. If you celebrate each milestone and pat yourself on the back for everything you're doing, you'll be motivated to keep going. You can do this, so believe in yourself and be prepared for the road ahead.

The Role of Parents as Allies and Partners

If there's a speck of dirt on your friend's shirt, you may pull them to the side and discreetly tell them, *"Hey, you have something on your shirt."* Or you might even choose not to mention it. But if you see the same thing on your brother's shirt, chances are you'll jump at the chance to use it to knock him down a little. You might say something like, *"Hey, dummy! Did you mop the floor with your shirt?"* After all, he's your brother. You've known him all his life, and you both play this game all the time. He won't take it as personally as a stranger would.

When it comes to the people we see every day, it's easy to cast aside the niceties we use for others in the name of familiarity, efficiency, and intimacy. But if you're struggling with mental health, it's worth remembering that your family members are there for you; they have your back, they are on your side, and they will never stop rooting for your growth and healing. This is why it's important to consider involving your family, especially your parents, when using DBT.

> **The most significant modification to DBT for teens is the inclusion in sessions of caregivers, parents, and other family members.** With caregivers involved, teens see great improvements in therapy because there may be issues at home that interfere with treatment, and with the inclusion of family, those issues can be addressed and solved.

The role of parents can never be underrated. In the teenage years, your parents are important sources of support and understanding as you grow. They're a shoulder to cry on and will always have your back, no matter the situation.

One very important role of parents is to understand what the therapy is truly about. It isn't a conventional method of trying to fix the issues of the children when they occur, but rather, it gives them the skills they need to face their emotional problems, deal with stress, and improve their relationships. When parents understand this, they are no longer dictators but partners with their children as they grow through this phase of life.

For parents, this is a win-win situation, because they can try out these DBT skills in their homes. Just as when we learn a new language, we try to use it to constantly improve, we can use DBT skills to steadily improve our abilities. In addition to partnering with their children as they grow, parents can also use the DBT skills on themselves to face whatever challenges life throws at them.

For parents in DBT, active listening is non-negotiable. So many teenagers feel they're never understood or heard, and this triggers unwanted behaviors in them. But when parents actively listen and try to understand their perspectives without judging or interrupting them, it gives the teens a deep sense of validation, and they feel important.

Parents can benefit tremendously from DBT. In fact, some of the programs include sessions specially made for parents, offering an excellent opportunity to learn more about the therapy and howas guardians they can offer support to their teens.

Parents should ensure that they're good examples of whatever they preach to their teens. Obviously, this makes the process easier, because when teens see these skills exhibited by their parents, they're more likely to absorb them. This means that if parents handle stress and emotions skillfully and healthily, they become positive role models for teens.

Chapter 2
Mindfulness for DBT

Every day, teens are faced with complex emotional and mental challenges as they try to comprehend an increasingly complex world influenced by social media, academic expectations, family dynamics, and the pressure to look and be perfect. Adding to these pressures is the still-in-progress development of the ability to manage stressors and balance changing responsibilities, making mindfulness a valuable skill every teen should learn.

There's no doubt that the teenage stage comes with problems that can make you feel totally lost, like everything is turning against you, and nothing seems to work. Why not try mindfulness and find out if it works?

> Mindfulness is not simply sitting alone and staring into space, thinking about nothing. It is an intentional act that will help you relax and calm your mind when confronted with a problem. It can help you see your present state, remain calm, and find a way through whatever difficulty you're experiencing.

This chapter will discuss mindfulness, similar to what Buddhist monks do when they meditate to attain a state of peace. You will see how powerful the act is and how you can explore your thoughts and feelings without being overwhelmed by them.

What is Mindfulness?

Mindfulness is the act of giving the present moment your full, undivided attention without judgment or overthinking. It entails responding to an emotion or situation thoughtfully rather than reacting impulsively. For teenagers who struggle with intense emotions, mindfulness can help them approach each situation and make an appropriate and effective choice.

You can do almost anything mindfully: eating, driving, fishing, journaling, painting. Still, certain mindfulness practices work better for teens, including body scans, grounding, and paced breathing, all of which we'll discuss.

Being mindful means prioritizing the present moment without tainting it with the past or the future and always being nonjudgmental. Most of us tend to judge our thoughts and feelings, but simply being aware of what we're thinking and feeling can be life-changing.

Think about that song you can sing word for word, beat for beat, and even mimic every instrument used. The reason you have so much knowledge about that song is that you have been mindful whenever you've heard it. You've listened to every detail and unconsciously know every bit of it. That's mindfulness. Regardless of what's happening around you, you find a way to key into the song and become one with it.

Why is this mindfulness important?

Sometimes, it can feel like your life is moving too fast, and you are trying your best to catch up. Mindfulness allows you to hit the pause button. Once you do this, you're able to slow down, catch your breath, and stay present and focused before having to return to reality.

Mindfulness is an effective antidote for stress and anxiety. You'll be much less likely to feel overwhelmed by your emotions or worries than someone who doesn't practice it. You'll be able to deal with tough situations and heavy emotions calmly.

The most amazing part of mindfulness is that you don't need any special location, equipment, or even requirements. It can be done anywhere and at any time. Bring your focus back to the present moment and ensure you're there – fully and completely, with no distractions.

Benefits of a Mindful Lifestyle

Because mindfulness allows you to step back and think before you act, you can apply it to many situations in your daily life. What's more, it works on all types of temperaments. You'll become more aware of your surroundings and emotions, which can lead to greater insight and better choices. Remember, observing *without judgment* is the foundation of mindfulness, and learning to understand yourself builds greater self-compassion and kindness.

In a world of endless notifications and constant distractions, concentration can be challenging. However, mindfulness requires sustained focus, which can help you develop your ability to concentrate. Because it teaches you to stop and take a thoughtful break before reacting impulsively, you'll improve your positive behaviors at school and home. You'll be less likely to react without thinking and instead use the skills you've learned in DBT to respond appropriately to every moment.

Mindfulness skills will boost your mental health by improving your awareness and teaching you to process your surroundings, emotions, and the situations you find yourself in thoughtfully rather than ignoring uncomfortable feelings and difficult emotions. This is how you develop strong mental health and skills that will benefit you for a lifetime.

Studies show that mindfulness can benefit teens in a number of ways, including:
- Developing optimism
- Encouraging better social behaviors
- Increasing attention spans
- Gaining self-control
- Decreasing anxiety
- Building self-compassion
- Improving emotion regulation

There's a wide range of mindfulness exercises in DBT that can strengthen your skills. Most exercises are simple and can be completed in a few minutes, and many have the added benefits of stress management and relaxation. Try to practice mindfulness exercises at least once a day to master the skills.

Many who practice mindfulness will talk about the tremendous impact it has had on their lives, but what is the science behind its effectiveness? The National Institutes of Health (NIH) reports that mindfulness meditation is powerful enough to change the concentration of gray matter in our brains, particularly in areas associated with learning, emotion regulation, and perspective (National Institutes of Health, 2010).

Another study by Harvard Medical School showed that meditation not only increased activity in the brain areas associated with the critical skills already mentioned, but it also significantly reduced activity in the amygdala, which is responsible for fear and stress (Harvard Gazette, 2018).

Experts are increasingly recommending mindfulness meditation as the first line of treatment for teens struggling with mental health issues. In fact, one study showed that mindful meditation can be just as effective at resolving the symptoms of certain mental health conditions as prescription drugs (Tanner L., 2022).

Mindfulness from a DBT Perspective

Mindfulness is a key component of emotion regulation in DBT treatment. You will begin each session with mindfulness because all other emotion regulation skills in DBT rely on your ability to be mindful.

> Though mindfulness is the act of recognizing when your thoughts wander and bringing them back to the present moment, it's also about looking at your thoughts without judgment. You'll have to learn the art of non-judgmental, present-focused awareness. You'll learn to listen to your thoughts, feelings, and actions without engaging in self-invalidation that leads to emotional dysregulation.

Many of us tend to spend hours not thinking about what we're doing or what's happening around us. We've become conditioned to engage with our thoughts rather than the reality we are living in, so we lose sight of what's happening around us, and this affects our ability to handle problems.

DBT prioritizes the treatment of emotional dysregulation, which is the root cause of many mental health issues. People may become emotionally dysregulated because of things that seem trivial, but this often happens because of our judgment of the event.

For example, you may like your school and your friends there. But maybe you don't like gym class because you get nothing out of it. You may only be required to participate in gym class for one hour every other day, which is a small percentage of everything you do in school. But when you're in gym class, your mind starts to wander. *I hate this. I'm so terrible at this; it's embarrassing. This is a complete waste of time, and these exercises are awful!*

Rather than staying focused on the activities you're doing, your mind is busy telling you negative stories about what you're doing. These thoughts then trigger negative emotions like resentment, anger, and hopelessness. What's worse is that these emotions seep into the rest of your day, ruining it altogether. Instead of dealing with a single hour of unpleasant exercise, you end up in a bad mood for the entire day, judging everything else negatively and feeling worse by the minute.

You begin thinking, *This is too much! I can't take it anymore. I hate this school!* So what started as a simple, insignificant thing has brought about a disproportionate amount of suffering.

A mindful approach to this scenario would be to view the unpleasant exercise with an attitude of acceptance and engage in it willingly, without overthinking or judging it. The moment a judgmental thought comes up, you would return your mind back to the exercise. Focus on your movements, your breathing, and the feelings that arise. When you fully immerse yourself in the present task, repeatedly turning your mind to it, there is less room for distraction and negative thought patterns. Soon, you may even find that the activity calms and soothes you.

This is just one example of how you can use mindfulness to avert negative thought patterns and emotional downward spirals.

Mindfulness can also improve your decision-making capabilities. Most people who struggle with extreme and pervasive emotional dysregulation have histories of their wants being invalidated, their emotions being neglected, and their ideas being overlooked. Eventually, this persistent invalidation gets to them, and they start to suffer on the inside. Soon enough, they invalidate their own feelings and experiences, having been conditioned to think that their emotions are bad or wrong.

When we do this time and again, we start to lose touch with our own experiences. We no longer listen to our own opinions or intuition, and end up not knowing what's best for us, and that's a terrible way to live.

Mindfulness in DBT will help you renounce your desire to control all your emotions. One of the main reasons people become emotionally dysregulated is that they try to ignore or control their emotional responses. But trying to control your emotions is like trying to grab Jello — the more you try, the messier it becomes. Similarly, the longer you try, the more intense the emotions become and the more likely they are to persist.

But when you're so used to being invalidated, there's a great deal of outside pressure controlling your emotions, which leads to even more intense emotions and then more self-invalidation. This becomes a self-perpetuating negative feedback loop.

> When you choose to be mindful of your emotions, you rise above that control strategy. With mindfulness, you watch your emotions from the outside. You become an observer. Yes, you noticed your cheek flush pink. You noticed a lump in your throat. You are keen on all these experiences, and your goal isn't to suppress them. Rather, it is to accept every emotion unconditionally. There's an old proverb that says, "It's impossible to argue with an emotion." This is true, because emotions arise for a reason. The best thing you can do is tolerate them instead of trying to push them away or control them.
>
> While this approach may seem like a paradox, I believe it's worth it. Eventually, the emotional experiences become less disturbing and shorter in duration. They go away just as naturally as they arrive. When you give them permission to exist and accept their natural fleeting course, you can overcome them. This is exactly why DBT skills rely heavily on mindfulness.

Mindfulness isn't easy to master, though. Our brains are conditioned from a young age to jump to conclusions, make judgments, worry, ruminate, cook up stories, and travel in time. In many ways, trying to be mindful is like working against your body's natural inclinations. No one has perfected this yet. But that shouldn't be the goal; you don't need to perfect it. You can experience the benefits of mindfulness once you learn to notice when your mind is wandering and choose to switch it back to the present moment. In other words, the real power of mindfulness is learning to recognize when you aren't being mindful!

If you are distracted a million times, you have a million opportunities to notice this and turn your mind back to the present moment. Think of it like fly fishing. Your mind may throw its line far off into the distance when you are distracted, but when you reel it back in, you ground yourself and reorient your thoughts to where they should be. This can happen a hundred times in a single minute. Like fly fishing, it happens continuously, and the more you practice, the better you get at it.

Mindfulness Exercises

Let's get practical with some mindfulness exercises you can infuse into your daily routine as a teenager. These exercises are simple, engaging, and relatable, and will fit into whatever type of schedule you have.

1. STOP

This pattern is a powerful mindfulness tool that comes in very handy when you feel overwhelmed by your emotions. When you feel your emotions taking control, STOP! Don't move. Freeze your muscles, don't react. Just STOP!

What does it mean to STOP?

S - Stop: Put a stop to whatever you're doing to avoid any impulsive reactions. Just like pilots land planes when there's an emergency, you should also land your emotions by halting whatever you're doing. This pause stops you from doing things you may later regret.

T - Take a Step Back: Once you've halted your activities, withdraw yourself from the triggering situation. Give yourself some space to catch your breath and assess the situation objectively and logically without sentiments. Change your point of view and replay the scene. This gives you a different view of what happened and reduces the expected intensity of such emotion.

O - Observe: After stopping and taking a step back, carefully look around and observe what's going on in your environment. Note what thoughts are running through your mind and how you feel at the moment. Try to identify the triggers behind these situations and know the 'why.' This will give you a sense of clarity, and you'll feel less intimidated by similar situations.

P - Proceed Mindfully: Now, you're in a mental space to be mindful. At this point, you have to make a conscious choice about how you react. Ensure you do the most helpful thing and react thoughtfully and not impulsively. This gives you more control over how you respond to challenging situations and emotions. As simple as it sounds, this is one of the most effective ways to handle stressful situations.

2. RAIN

Just like STOP, RAIN is another effective technique. It helps to deal with intense and difficult situations. What does RAIN stand for?

R - Recognize: When tough times come, no headway can be achieved without first doing a thorough investigation to know what you're experiencing. You have to acknowledge the feelings, thoughts, and sensations that are present. They can be positive or negative. Once you recognize what the issue is, you're on the right track to putting an end to similar situations or experiences.

A - Allow: Allow the identified experience to just be. Don't attempt to judge or even change it. This is a tough one, but give yourself the room to feel whatever emotion you're feeling at that moment in time.

I - Investigate: Now that you've given yourself permission to feel the relevant emotion of the present situation, gently investigate to find out why you feel the way you do. Don't overanalyze. Understand 'why' and what made you feel this way. This will go a long way toward making things better.

N - Non-Identification: This is the last step in RAIN, and it simply tells you to consciously remind yourself that you are not your thoughts or emotions. These are just experiences that must come and go. You have to define yourself by not detaching from how you feel or how you've felt in the past. A little shift in perspective is very important, as it can make a huge difference in how you relate to your emotions.

When you use the RAIN technique, you give yourself time to process what's going on within yourself before reacting. If you're the type who reacts immediately to issues, try this out. When you have some sense of control over your emotions, it allows you to react with more clarity and wisdom, which helps creates peace, understanding, and kindness, all of which can prevent future problems.

3. Mindful Eating

Consider being mindful while you eat. Do it slowly and thoughtfully instead of rushing through your meal. Pay attention and avoid distractions and you'll likely enjoy your food even more.

You can do this with anything you eat throughout the day, but let's practice with an apple. Feel free to do it with your eyes closed if it helps.

- Feel the apple and roll it around in your hand. How does it feel?
- Bring the apple close to your nose. How does it smell? Take a whiff of the sweet scent.
- If you have your eyes open, examine the apple closely. Is the skin smooth? Is the color even? Is it firm or squishy?
- Taste the apple. How does it feel on your tongue? How does it feel against your teeth? What about the flavor? The texture? Is it juicy?
- Chew the apple slowly. Take your time and notice the smell and taste with each bite.

4. Mindful Breathing

There are multiple ways to do mindful breathing. It can be done whether you're breathing slowly or quickly. The goal is for you to pay attention to your breathing and not do it in a forced way.

Here's how:

- Sit upright in a chair. Make sure you're comfortable. Close your eyes.
- Pay attention to your breathing. Inhale and exhale slowly. Pay attention to the inhale. Can you feel the air as it passes through your nostrils?
- Pay attention to the exhale. Does your breath go out of your nostrils gently or roughly? Is your chest moving as you do this? What about your belly?
- Do nothing for a few minutes except pay attention to your breathing. Does this relax you?

That's the power of mindfulness. It can calm you down while you are merely sitting there. If your mind starts to wander, try to guide it back to the breath.

As you continue to grow through this teenage phase, don't forget that mindfulness is meant for anyone conscious and willing to practice it. Don't give up. Keep trying and pushing, and don't be too harsh with yourself during this process. Hopefully, this chapter has encouraged you to incorporate mindfulness into your daily life.

Chapter 3
Emotion Regulation

Our teenage years come with so many emotional loads, it can become worrisome. Sometimes, you find yourself escaping one emotional moment and facing another almost instantly. What do you do when you experience a situation like this? That's where emotion regulation comes into play. Emotion regulation isn't about putting a stop to these emotions but acknowledging them, living with them, and excelling in spite of them.

In this chapter, we'll discusses what emotions are and learn techniques to help you properly respond to yours. By the end of the chapter, you'll be equipped for all those times when you feel like your emotions are controlling you.

We'll also talk about how to identify emotional triggers, how to relax before reacting, and, most importantly, how to express your feelings without hurting others. Consider this chapter a guide to learning a new skill to improve your emotional health.

No matter the stage of life you find yourself in, your emotions remain relevant and useful.

Understanding Your Emotions

Every emotion you experience is attached to a specific piece of information linked to your experiences and reactions. When anxiety creeps in, there might be an issue somewhere that needs attention. The same thing applies to positive emotions like happiness. When you feel happy, there's an experience attached to it. When you see emotions as meaningful signals rather than random happenings, you're on the road to taking control of how you react to them.

Try to paint a mental picture of a board with segments marked off in different colors. Every segment and its color represents a feeling. These feelings include joy, anger, sadness, fear, jealousy, pride, relief, and every other human emotion. Trace each emotion you feel to the right segment on your picture board when they occur. This gives you an insight into your emotional world and helps you figure out what exactly is happening.

Identifying physical indicators is also an important factor when it comes to understanding your emotions. Our body usually reacts to the sensations each emotion carries. When you're scared, your heart beats faster, and when you feel joy, you might feel 'butterflies' in your belly. These are physical ways your body indicates various emotions. When you know your system and how it works in connection with your emotions, you have more information when physical indicators arise.

It's also crucial to be attentive to your triggers. Look inward deeply and identify those things that trigger your emotions. These could be situations, people, or thoughts that spark certain emotions in you. Practice mindfulness, identify the triggers, and note them down. Whenever you sense the triggers coming your way, your knowledge of them will make it easier to avoid them, and even when they are unavoidable, you're at least prepared for what's coming.

Naturally, the intensity of emotions varies from person to person. Some may be overwhelming for you and not for someone else. Be aware of the intensity of your emotions, and you will manage and respond to them as you should.

Remember to avoid negative thinking. Thoughts are huge influencing factors when it comes to your emotional state. If you think positively, you'll almost surely experience positive emotions. When you consciously divert your thoughts down a positive route, the results are always beneficial. The formula is simple: positive thoughts = positive feelings, negative thoughts = negative feelings.

Emotions are transient. They flow with no particular destination, and they come and go. Once you can think of them like this, you're more resilient, even in the face of the most intense emotions. Emotions allow us to experience life in all its richness but uncontrolled emotions can cause us enormous distress and suffering. Learning how to regulate your emotions is one of the most important skills you can master to live a fulfilling life.

Emotion regulation is a skill that helps us understand how our emotions function. An 'action urge' goes along with each emotion, whether you act on it or oppose it. This teaches us how to deal with emotions. For example, how to pause and gather our thoughts before responding. Emotion regulation can also mean waiting until you're in a supportive environment so you can handle difficult emotions. **Emotion regulation is vital for mental health and for establishing and maintaining good relationships. It helps you understand that emotions are an important part of your life.**

DBT teaches you how to deal with your emotions,, which can be subject to frequent changes and be particularly strong in anyone who suffers from emotional dysregulation. People with emotional dysregulation frequently behave in ways that are intended to alleviate their discomfort or legitimize their feelings. This can lead to actions that are more damaging.

Learning to regulate emotions is a central part of DBT. This doesn't mean the emotions are invalid or unimportant, and you are not trying to rid yourself of them entirely. They are valid, important, and natural. But because they can cause so much pain and often make you feel out of control, they need to be managed. Part of that is recognizing emotions, validating them, and accepting them as real and meaningful.

Identifying Your Emotions

This is an important step in managing your emotions. It can be difficult, especially when you're feeling overwhelmed or confused, particularly during your teenage years, when you're experiencing so many new and intense emotions. But it's important to put a name to your feelings so you can understand them better and develop healthy coping mechanisms.

Below are useful tips to help you recognize different emotional states:

- **Observe:** One way to help you label your feelings is by taking note of how adults in your life express their own. For example, a parent who just received a promotion might say, *"I'm excited and proud of myself for working so hard."*
- **Journal:** Use a journal or notebook to write about your everyday experiences and how you feel. Reviewing previous entries can help you recognize patterns in your feelings.
- **Discuss:** Don't be ashamed to talk with others about how you feel.
- **Learn the language:** When discussing emotions with peers and parents, try to use specific emotion-related words like "happy," "sad," "angry," "scared," "excited," and "frustrated." This will improve your understanding of emotional language.

As humans, it can be difficult for us to identify exactly what we feel. It can be challenging to fit emotions into categories because of how complex they are. But try to pay attention and be more aware of your emotional self. This awareness is a secret weapon to aid your learning of regulating and managing your emotions.

Challenging Negative Thought Patterns

When we feel pessimistic about something or we think irrationally, we develop negative thought patterns that aren't good for our emotional health. This affects our perspective of life, leading to stress, anxiety, and depression.

You can't achieve emotion regulation without challenging your negative thought patterns. When you do so, you reduce the influence they have on your feelings and behaviors.

Learn to pinpoint and challenge those negative thoughts, and you'll change how you respond emotionally. You're probably wondering how you can do this, so let's find out.

• Question the Validity

The moment you sense a negative thought, question the validity of it in your mind. Is the thought really true? Or are you just being emotional? Examine the circumstances surrounding the thought and come to a logical conclusion. This will help you separate the truth from imagination.

• Consider Alternative Explanations

There are always at least two sides to a problem. Remember this when you have negative thoughts. Your thoughts are probably leaning toward the pessimistic rather than the best-case scenario. Try to see the positive side of whatever experience has caused you concern. That negative conclusion you've arrived at may not actually be true or accurate.

- **Mindfulness and Acceptance**

Mindfulness is a skill that teaches us to calmly observe our thought patterns without allowing them to take control of us. Start by accepting the reality that those negative thoughts are normal, and they may not be factual. They are thoughts that will always come and go, but never allow them to have power over you and your reactions.

- **Keep a Thought Diary**

Whenever negative thought patterns manifest, pick up your diary and note them down along with everything surrounding the occurrence. Don't skip any details. Follow this with a corresponding positive or balanced thought beside each negative one. This is a good way to help challenge negative thoughts.

- **Seek Evidence**

When negative thoughts occur, look for solid evidence that opposes them. If you think you're bad at school, check your records and ask yourself again if you really are doing poorly in school. Write down all the positive times you've excelled and counter the negative thoughts.

- **Talk to Yourself Like a Friend**

This technique involves role-playing. Picture yourself as one of your friends who shares the same negative thoughts with you. What would you advise them to do? Unfortunately, we tend to be harsher toward ourselves than we are to others. Whatever you say to your friend, say it to yourself and put it into practice.

- **Professional Guidance**

If you've tried all the above tactics and nothing seems to work, consider seeking help from a mental health professional, as they are trained to support people with similar issues.

Overcoming negative thought patterns doesn't happen overnight. It requires a lot of patience and consistency. But little by little, you can make progress, and the strategies will become a part of your life.

Building Emotional Resilience

Emotional resilience is the ability to cope with difficult emotions and bounce back from setbacks. It doesn't do away with stress or eliminate life's difficulties but instead allows you to handle and accept life's problems. It is a vital skill to develop during your teenage years, as you are often faced with challenges like academic pressure, social conflicts, and family problems.

Here are some tips for building emotional resilience:

- **Take Care of Yourself**

When it comes to your physical and mental well-being, self-care isn't negotiable. Prioritize it by engaging in activities that refresh you and put you in good shape emotionally. It might also mean eating healthy foods, getting enough sleep, and exercising regularly.

Learn from Your Mistakes

We all make mistakes. But when we learn from these mistakes, we take valuable lessons from them. Don't think of mistakes as setbacks but as opportunities to grow and further develop yourself. Everyone makes mistakes; learn from yours and move on instead of dwelling on them.

Set Boundaries

As a teen, you should know your limits, needs, and the things you prefer. When you learn to set boundaries, you're indirectly aiding your self-care and building paths to healthy relationships. If others have unreasonable expectations or require too much of you, learn to set boundaries.

Practice Acceptance

The reality is that stress and pain are natural parts of life. Recognize your pain, knowing that it will pass, and you will survive. Think about what you can change and what you can't.

Connect with Others

No one is an island; you shouldn't dwell in isolation. When you engage with people around you, you will likely find support, joy, and a sense of relevance and belonging. Spending time with people you care about, receiving support, and talking about challenging issues can help you feel more positive and keep things in perspective.

Emotion Regulation Exercises

We all hope to maintain a mental balance and well-being. But this is impossible without emotional regulation, which helps us manage and properly respond to our emotions in a healthy way. Following are some practical exercises you can practice to achieve this.

1. Opposite Action

Emotions often cause reactions, most of which are biologically wired. Many times, we give in to our emotions, doing exactly what they want us to do. Overcoming this urge and choosing to do the opposite of what your emotions are pushing you to do is a critical skill.

Emotions are always accompanied by a behavior. Your body is biologically wired to make you react to emotion in a certain way. For example, when you're angry, you might feel the urge to argue.

Initial Emotion	Urge	Opposite Action	Opposite Emotion
Anger	Attack, yell, argue, be judgmental	Gently avoid, be kind, validate, use a soft voice	**Calmness**
Fear	Hunch shoulders, avoid, freeze	Approach what you fear, seek support in coping with it	**Brave, confident**
Shame/guilt	Self-destruct, avoidance, negative self-talk	Positive self-talk, self-compassion	**Feeling worthwhile, useful**
Sadness	Isolate, withdraw, cry	Be active, reach out to friends or loved ones	**Happy, engaged**
Frustration	Blame others, give up, move on	Take responsibility, try again, take a break	**Confidence**

Opposite actions help you change your emotions. If you are tempted to yell to make a point when you're angry, try doing the opposite by speaking calmly and politely.

2. Checking the Facts

Checking the facts will help you evaluate whether your emotions and their intensity match the facts of the situation. This will help you become adept at changing your emotional responses. First, learn to pause and check the facts before acting. This encourages you to consider alternative interpretations or explanations for distressing events and challenge yourself to formulate alternative explanations by considering different perspectives.

Below is a simple exercise to help you check the facts:

What emotions am I experiencing?

How intense is the emotion on a scale of 1–10?

What is the situation that triggered the emotion?

What are my thoughts/interpretations/assumptions of the situation? How can adding to the facts change how I feel?

Have I allowed any negative thoughts to distract me from the facts of the situation?

Does the intensity of what I am feeling fit the facts of the situation?

Can I do away with the intensity of the emotions, interpretations, and distractions and rewrite my initial description of the prompting event with only verifiable facts? What happened was…

3. PLEASE

Your body and mind are linked, and the health of one directly affects the other. **PLEASE** is an acronym to help you remember a set of skills to regulate emotions. It helps you take care of your basic needs in order to make better decisions and be less vulnerable to emotional disruption.

PL: Physical health

Take care of your body and see a doctor when you're not feeling well. Take prescribed medication as directed.

E: Eat

Eat food that nourishes your body to promote better health. Don't overeat or eat too little. Avoid meals that make you feel overly emotional and that fill without giving you energy.

A: Avoid mood-altering substances

Avoid any substance that changes the way you feel about things. Stay off non-prescribed drugs, including alcohol, and beware of your caffeine and sugar intake.

S: Sleep

An unhealthy sleep schedule can throw you off balance. Try to get enough sleep and create a sleep schedule if you have difficulty sleeping. Too little sleep can make you vulnerable to negative emotions like depression.

E: Exercise

Engage in some physical activity that stimulates chemical reactions in your brain that bring about a happier mood. 15 minutes of daily exercise should do the trick!

4. Emotion Regulation Toolkit

Sometimes, strong emotions feel overwhelming and difficult to deal with. Preparing your emotional toolkit for such moments can really help you deal with difficult emotions. It's important to have a variety of tools so you can choose the ones that work best for you in different situations.

What can you include in an emotional toolkit?

• Positive affirmations

You can write positive affirmations and post them, or you can watch positive affirmation videos and repeat them to yourself every morning. This aids in the formation of positive beliefs. If you do this every day, you will feel stronger and more capable of dealing with difficult situations when they occur.

• Meditation

Practicing meditation every day can transform your outlook on life. It can help you live a more serene existence by instilling in you a sense of calm. There are multiple methods to do this: You can follow a guided meditation video, sit quietly, or sit listening to soothing music or sounds of nature.

- **Talk to someone**

Having a loved one we can talk to about how we're feeling helps us feel less alone and gives us an outlet through which to express ourselves.

- **Take a walk**

Exercise benefits both mental and physical health, since it allows you to clear your thoughts, get some fresh air, and move your body, all at the same time. You can also soak in Vitamin D from the sun, which is essential for mental wellness!

- **Read a book or listen to an audiobook**

Books help us escape reality and enter another world, thereby distracting us from challenging emotions.

Any skill can be mastered when it is practiced with patience and consistency. Emotion regulation is no exception. Be patient with yourself as you do these exercises. With time, you'll notice you have a better grip on your emotions.

Chapter 4

Distress Tolerance

Life can be like living somewhere with all sorts of weather conditions, from calm and sunny, to stormy, to high winds to freezing rain. As a teen, it's crucial to keep your head up no matter the intensity of the weather, so tolerance is an important skill to master.

This chapter discusses distress tolerance and how to make proper use of this skill in the face of various challenges life may throw at you. We'll review every tool you need to help you manage any distress.

Trying to avoid the problems of life is impossible, but understanding your environment and the factors surrounding distress is not. Let's explore ways to spot an emotionally disturbing moment on time and how to cope with it.

Understanding Distress and Its Impact

Distress Tolerance is the core of DBT, and it's focused on stressful events. While the other skills are helpful in all sorts of situations and generally make life easier, distress tolerance skills increase an individual's ability to tolerate emotionally charged events. Whenever you feel stressed, anxious, or worried, distress tolerance skills are exactly what you need to calm yourself.

> Distress tolerance skills are divided into two categories: crisis survival and reality acceptance. The former helps us deal with critical events, while the latter helps us accept reality. They also teach us the importance of learning from these situations so the next time something unpleasant happens, we're not upset or hurt again.

There is no denying that the teenage years come with high stress levels. You need these skills to endure and to avoid acting on impulse in stressful situations. For example, maybe you accidentally trip at school, and everyone around you starts laughing. This would likely make you feel embarrassed and angry, and your urge might be to punch someone who's laughing at you. If you give in to it, you'll be in trouble. If you don't give in to it, you may be stewing in embarrassment for days, but distress tolerance will help you tolerate the situation and move on quickly.

Physical Impact of Distress

It is almost impossible to have emotional problems without experiencing some physical effects.

The physical impact of distress varies for each individual. Some might get a headache, while others develop digestive problems. When this becomes persistent, it begins to weaken the immune system, which can make you sick.

In the same way a battery's power weakens when you overuse it or overload it, the body reacts when emotional stress becomes overwhelming. You start to notice signs, and if you're not careful, things may get out of hand and negatively impact your body.

Whenever you feel stressed, be aware that at some point, your body will react. To combat the physcial affects, be sure to take good care of yourself physically and mentally. When the battery on our phone or laptop is low, we re-charge it, right? Do the same for your body.

Mental and Emotional Effects

Life is filled with ups and downs, and when the downs come, emotions fluctuate, and this can lead to anxiety. As anxiety operates on one end, sadness operates on another. You may feel like you're carrying a heavy invisible burden. This affects every aspect of life because, after a while, it can make you irritable. The smallest things might annoy you, and you start snapping at things that would not catch your attention on a normal day.

All this can make it difficult to maintain balance. You strive to move on, but because you're experiencing many different things at once, negativity creeps in. You see more negatives than positives around you and might even begin to feel hopeless. You may feel stuck in a loop of negative thoughts and feel like things will never get better. This stage is normal because bad times are a part of life.

Don't make matters worse by immersing yourself in these feelings. Take action to get yourself out. One method is to talk to a trusted friend or your parents.

Behavioral Changes

There are behavioral patterns that can tell you when you're experiencing distress. You might realize that you've been isolating yourself from friends and family. Maybe activities you do for fun or relaxation suddenly seem uninteresting, and you begin to doubt yourself. You don't get quality sleep like you used to, or you start to oversleep beyond what is normal for you. All these are behavioral signals that something is wrong.

Some people resort to coping habits like eating junk food, drinking alcohol, or taking drugs to escape from all the stress and emotional hurt. But this path will only worsen the problems and won't bring relief.

Remember, these changes in behavior are warning signs on your emotional dashboard. They're indicating that something isn't right and you need to take care of your emotional health. It's important to address these indicators early so you can more quickly and easily get back on track. Don't allow distress to last long before you tackle it because it can lead to mental issues like anxiety disorders or depression. It also impacts your relationships, performance at work, academics, quality of life, and general well-being.

How to Cope with Distress
(Health Coping Strategies)

When we feel stressed, we use certain strategies to feel better. It's also important that we have strategies to cope with distress. Following are ways that can help you cope with distress.

- **Get Moving**

This is an underrated tool to combat distress. When distress rears its ugly head, pause what you're doing and become physically active. Take a walk or bike ride, dance to your favorite music, do some exercises, anything that gets your body moving. This will almost certainly benefit your mood.

Sports lovers know the feeling of satisfaction that comes when we play our favorite sport. We become immersed in the rhythm of the game, and before we know it, our mind is no longer thinking about whatever distress we were in, because we're focusing on the game.

Dancers can relate, too. It's almost impossible to be sad while you're dancing. This activity tends to create a deep feeling of happiness and joy, which is the perfect medicine for distress.

So the next time you start to feel any sign of distress, get moving and have fun. Trust me, it works!

- **Use Relaxation Techniques**

Relaxation in the midst of chaos may sound impossible. But there are various relaxation techniques to help you cope with distress. Breathing exercises, either alone or with the aid of apps, are one of these techniques. A long, warm bath is another effective solution you might consider.

The **TIPP** skills are a set of four distress tolerance skills that can be used to provide immediate relief from distress. The following explains this acronym:

○ **T - Temperature:**
This skill involves using temperature to shock your system out of emotional distress. There are several techniques you might employ for relief, such as splashing cold water on your face. The shock of cold triggers the dive reflex, which can temporarily interrupt intense emotion. Or you might take a hot bath, sit with a heating pad, or have a hot cup of tea. The hot water can restore your heart rate to a regular rhythm when you're in distress.

○ **I - Intense exercise:**
Engaging in a brief, high-intensity workout, like jogging, can help release pent-up emotional energy and provide immediate relief.

○ **P - Paced breathing:**
Paced breathing focuses on slowing down your breath. Breathe in deeply for a count of four, hold for four, and exhale for four. This controlled breathing pattern can help calm your nervous system and reduce emotional intensity.

○ **P - Progressive muscle relaxation:**
This technique entails tensing and then relaxing various muscle groups throughout your body. Begin with your feet and work your way up to your head. This procedure relieves physical tension and promotes relaxation.

- **Explore Creative Outlets**

There are times when you might be able to intentionally reverse the affects of distress by turning it into something awesome. Have you tried pouring out your emotions into artwork and seeing what comes out of it? You might even end up creating a masterpiece using this therapeutic approach!

Words do it for some people – those who love writing might be amazed at how eloquently they're able to pour out their hearts and thoughts when they experience distress. Anything from writing poems or stories to keeping a journal would work. When thoughts and emotions are put into words, it can be a tremendous relief. And when the storm of feelings has passed, you may wish to go back and read what you wrote to help you find some clarity.

Music is another method people use to express themselves. It's almost magical the way it can influence moods. Pick up that instrument or listen to your favorite playlist and watch your mood instantly improve.

Cooking and baking are also ways to cope with distress. Creating something from scratch can be really calming and satisfying. This is a positive way to keep your mind focused and productive.

The best part about exploring creative outlets is that there's no standard way to do it. Figure out what works for you and stick to it.

• Develop a Self-Care Routine

The importance of self-care cannot be overemphasized. Self-care means prioritizing yourself and engaging in activities that make you feel good. It might involve something as trivial as taking a walk, spending some time with people who make you happy, or even just getting a good night's sleep or taking a nap.

• Build a Support System

A support system is composed of those friends and family members who will always be there for you, and you can share your deepest desires and fears with them. They are your cheerleaders who are always pushing you and staying strong with you when things get tough. They can also be teachers, mentors, and guardians. They offer you a different perspective and advise you based on their experiences. There are also online communities and support groups you might choose to connect with. No matter how far they are physically, they are available in the virtual space and ready to encourage you to live your best life.

Professional mentors also play vital roles in the support system chain. These people offer services from a professional angle and help you stay focused. When things are difficult, they encourage you without judgment.

Support systems aren't just there when things aren't going well. They are also there for the good times. And you should not only be a receiver of support, but a giver as well. When you are there for others, it strengthens the bond you share with them. The end goal is to build a strong circle that thrives on positivity and unconditional support for one another.

Distress Tolerance Exercises

The following exercises are important when things get tough. You need them to help you get through the difficult phases without falling apart.

1. Radical Acceptance

Developing radical acceptance takes time and practice, and it isn't easy, but it's an important key to breaking free from unhappiness and finding peace. It's an effective way to embrace the reality of life as it is without resistance. It's worth the struggle when you consider the alternative, which is feeling like you're not in control.

The easiest way to develop this is to make an effort to change your usual way of thinking. When we encounter difficult situations, we often ask ourselves, *What if...? What if I fail the exams? What if I can't do it? What if they don't like me? To change such habitual negative thinking, consider alternative possibilities that support you instead.*

Use the worksheet below to help you accept the reality of a distressing situation:

I. Challenging situation

Identify and write down the distressing situation you're experiencing.

II. How did it make you feel?

Write down the emotions evoked by the event.

III. Thoughts/beliefs

Write down the thoughts you have about the situation.

IV. The reality

Write about the reality of the event as objectively as possible.

V. What can I change?

Identify what you can change about the situation.

2.　ACCEPTS

This set of skills can help you cope with an unpleasant emotion until you can address and ultimately resolve the situation.

Let's break it down:

A - Activities: Participate in any beneficial activity. Read a story, take a walk, call a friend, clean your room — anything that distracts you and keeps your mind off negative emotions. If you finish, switch to a different activity. (You could have a really productive day as you divert your attention away from that dreaded event!)

C - Contribution: Volunteer to help others, surprise a friend or family with something nice, donate to a cause, or do something to make someone happy. In other words, do something nice for someone else.

C - Comparison: Compare how you are feeling now to a time when you felt different in order to remind yourself that the situation isn't permanent. Think about people who might be going through the same thing as you or worse. Watch a TV show where others are experiencing similar issues.

E - Emotions: Do something intentional that will elicit a distinct, intense, or competing emotion. For example, feeling sad? Watch a comedy. Feeling nervous? Listen to calming music. Target an emotion that is positive or enjoyable to counter the emotion associated with distress.

P - Pushing away: If possible, leave the situation, and if not, distance yourself from whatever is causing you distress by temporarily pushing it out your mind. Build an imaginary wall between you and the situation and keep yourself from thinking about it until a later time. Keep postponing thinking about it.

T - Thoughts: Try to focus on your thoughts when your emotions take over. Distract yourself with unrelated thoughts, like counting to 10. When you focus on one thing, it makes it difficult to think about another.

S - Sensations: Focus on physical sensations, like holding an ice cube or drinking a hot cup of tea, to redirect your attention away from your emotions.

Worksheet

Triggering situation:

The ACCEPTS skill I tried was:

I chose the skill because:

The way I used this skill was:

Because of this skill, I was able to avoid the following reactions:

Was the skill successful?

3. Self-soothing

This technique helps calm you down when you're experiencing negative emotions. Using your body's senses is a simple technique to raise your discomfort tolerance in a crisis. Examples include stroking your pet, holding a stuffed animal, or wrapping yourself in your favorite blanket. This type of sensual self-soothing can quickly decrease the severity of negative feelings.

Sight: Focus your vision on something else. Count the number of times you see a specific color in the room, watch a beautiful sunset, or concentrate on the texture of an object. You might also take out your phone and scroll through your favorite images.

Hearing: Listen to sounds of any kind. Can you hear birds chirping or cars outside? Turn up the volume on your favorite song, and just listen. If you prefer relaxing noises, there are numerous apps that you could play while on the go.

Taste: A simple treat can provide you with something nice to focus on while you're going through a difficult time. You don't have to make a full meal; even a piece of gum or a few mints will suffice.

Smell: Focus on whatever aroma is in the air, whether it's good or unpleasant. Can you identify the smell or at least dissect it into its components? You might even put a few drops of essential oil onto a cotton ball and keep it in a plastic bag for convenient access to a calming aroma.

Movement: Your body's movements can influence your emotional state, so go for a walk or bike ride around the block or dance in your living room to your favorite song!

Distress is a natural part of life. You don't need to be scared of it or try to avoid it. Instead, accept it, understand it, and manage it. Practice everything this chapter has discussed, and you're ready to challenge distress to a fight and win.

Remember, most of this can't be achieved overnight; trust the process. Don't give up, and be consistent. It may become tougher at some point, but the end promises to be positive and rewarding.

Chapter 5
Interpersonal Effectiveness

Humans engage in social interactions almost constantly. Think of this chapter as your go-to guide through social interactions. Whether it's chatting with friends, dealing with family, or understanding the different personalities you encounter daily, you will learn how to manage these encounters like a pro.

You'll gain all the skills and techniques needed to communicate more clearly and handle conflicts as if you were professionally trained to do so. You will express your feelings, needs, and opinions without hurting anyone and become a good listener.

Understanding Interpersonal Effectiveness

Interpersonal effectiveness is the one-on-one exchange of emotions, feelings, thoughts, and ideas between two or more people. This includes direct verbal communication, non-verbal communication, empathy, and other forms of personal interaction. With interpersonal effectiveness skills, you can manage your relationships, find a balance between your demands and priorities, balance your 'shoulds' and 'wants,' and build an unshakeable sense of self-respect and self-confidence.

> The two main skills needed to master interpersonal effectiveness are communication and empathy. You'll also need to work on your patience, listening skills, self-awareness, conflict resolution, teamwork, leadership, and negotiation tactics.

People who lack interpersonal effectiveness skills often have a hard time relating to and empathizing with others, approach people with a "cool" attitude that only encourages an uncomfortable interaction, and can be arrogant and insensitive. They may appear distant, unapproachable, impatient, or intense. Some are too busy to pay attention, and even when they do, they are quick to move on to address their own agenda. They may dismiss or devalue others and demonstrate a lack of respect. They usually don't pay enough attention to understand others; rather, they tend to quickly jump to conclusions and judgments. They are direct and lack the skills necessary to "read" people and build rapport with them.

Emotional intelligence is the foundation of interpersonal effectiveness. This is the ability to be aware of your thoughts and feelings and how they impact others. Fortunately, interpersonal effectiveness can be learned; anyone can learn to work on their communication skills, how to manage disagreements, and how to reconcile differences with others.

Effective Communication Skills and Assertiveness

Healthy communication is powerful. It can turn a sour relationship into a positive one. Effective communication entails active listening, honesty, and respect. You need to open yourself up so others can understand what you want or need. Healthy communication isn't just limited to talking; listening is equally important.

It's easy to talk to others during good times when you and those you're conversing with are seeing eye to eye. But you also need to be able to talk about difficult issues without hurting or insulting one another or turning the conversation into an argument. You may not always agree, but you can talk through your differences respectfully so all parties feel heard. Effective communication isn't manipulative, disrespectful, or mean-spirited. It's not about getting your way; it's about being there for the people you care about.

So, how do we do this?

Identify Your Communication Style

Let's review the various communication styles to understand where you fall on the spectrum.

• Assertive Communication Style

People with an assertive communication style can clearly and honestly express their thoughts, emotions, and needs. They are self-aware, aware of the needs of others, and often try their best to compromise and accommodate them. They treat people respectfully when they communicate.

• Passive Communication Style

People with a passive communication style have a hard time expressing themselves. They often block out their thoughts and feelings. They are fearful that when they fully express themselves, they may trigger others, cause conflict, or create bad feelings between them and those around them.

Aggressive Communication Style

People with an aggressive communication style tend to prioritize their own needs and goals. Their desires come first, regardless of other people's needs. Often, they are verbally aggressive with others and may try to control them. Others end up feeling intimidated, bitter, and hurt.

Passive-Aggressive Communication Style

Passive-aggressive communicators have a hard time expressing themselves directly, but often do it indirectly. But they may not express their emotions clearly, leaving others confused or feeling like they are being manipulated.

Below, adapted from Sheri Van Dijk's book, *DBT Made Simple*, are the four styles of communication, with bulleted statements beneath each. Analyze the statements and think about which one suits you best. Circle the ones that are most characteristic of your communication style. This will help you develop a better understanding of the way you communicate.

Assertive

- I often feel like I can and am allowed to express myself to others. I can share with them my thoughts and feelings.
- I pay attention to my needs and those of others. I would say I am good at making compromises.
- I always listen carefully to others and think about what they are telling me. Also, I ensure they know I am listening to them.
- Whenever I am arguing with someone, I express my thoughts and emotions clearly and honestly.
- I respect myself. I treat others with respect and make them feel heard when communicating with them.

Passive

- If I express my thoughts and feelings, I know people will get angry or reject me.
- I don't like upsetting people, so I normally stay quiet.
- I often ignore my feelings instead of communicating them to others.
- Even when something matters to me, I rarely state it. I don't open up about issues I care about.
- I avoid the spotlight. Even when I have a different opinion, I'd rather not open up about what I think and have people's attention focused on me.

Aggressive

- Some of my friends feel intimidated by my presence.
- My needs and goals always come first, regardless of who is with or around me.
- I believe my way is always the right way.
- I swear and yell and can be verbally abusive at times.
- It's not my problem if the needs of people around me aren't being met.

Passive-Aggressive

- When I am angry at someone, I give them the silent treatment.
- Even when I want something different, I often agree to do things others want me to do.
- When I become angry, I might mock people to make them angry as well. I swear and yell and can be verbally abusive at times.
- I have a hard time expressing my emotions, but I may show anger in different ways.
- When I feel angry, I may try to tone it down so people won't reject me.

Now, think about how your communication style affects your relationships:

Does your communication style affect your relationships? If yes, how?

Think about your communication style and with whom you use it most often. Do you think there is room for improvement in the way you communicate?

Finally, think about whether your communication style is effective.

Tips to Improve Communication

Here are some tips to improve your communication:

- **Be assertive without being aggressive.**
  If you'd like to be more assertive but still come across as polite, try to let others speak first. If you interrupt someone, catch yourself and say, *"I'm sorry, please go ahead,"* and let them finish what they're saying.

  Ask the other person for their opinion and listen attentively. It's okay to disagree. What's not okay is to put others down or bash their point of view when you disagree with them. For example, instead of saying, *"That's a dumb idea,"* or *"You are such a jerk,"* try, *"I don't think that's right,"* or *"That's a little insensitive."*

  Think of someone you know who is an assertive communicator and follow their example. Think about their best qualities when communicating and, if you can, imitate them.

- **Use "I" statements.**
  Use "I' instead of "you," which sounds more accusatory. Say things like, "I feel angry when you..." instead of "You are making me angry." Steer clear of statements that sound like you are blaming others or imply that they are purposely trying to hurt you.

- **Be clear and direct.**
  This doesn't mean you should be rude, but remember, no one is a mind reader. If you don't tell people what you want or need, they won't know. Don't assume people know how you feel; it's your responsibility to tell them.

- **Don't bury your feelings.**
  Talk about things that bother you as early as you can, so they won't build up and make you resentful. When you talk about something that bothers you as soon as it occurs, you can prevent it from becoming a bigger problem.

- **Build trust.**
Unless you have a reason not to believe someone, always believe that they are telling you the truth. Assume they are being honest and mean well. This helps establish trust.

- **Ask questions.**
If someone says something that doesn't make sense or you don't understand, ask the them what they mean. Don't make assumptions.

- **If it's important, talk in person.**
You can easily be misunderstood or misinterpreted when you send a serious message via text or email. If you want to be understood, talk to the person face to face or via video call, or at least a voice call if these other options aren't possible. Your tone of voice and body language will reduce the chances of your words being misinterpreted.

- **Don't yell.**
It's okay to be angry or defensive during an argument, but don't use it as an excuse to shout at others. If you feel like you are too angry or upset, take a break from the conversation until you've cooled down, then return and talk about what happened.

- **Apologize.**
We all make mistakes. Say you're sorry when you're wrong, and mean it. Being apologetic when you're wrong can go a long way in helping you and the other person move on after a misunderstanding.

- **Say "no" respectfully.**
It can be hard to say no, even when you know it's the right thing to do. You may feel guilty or be afraid you'll come across as mean. You may be afraid to offend the other person or lose the relationship if you say no. These feelings can make it hard to be your true self, so you may end up feeling awkward and dishonest.

So, how can you say no as kindly as possible?

Be conscious of your body language. As explained earlier, communication isn't limited to words. Think about what it is you're communicating with your facial expressions; your face is probably the most communicative part of your body. If you want your "No" to be impactful, make sure it is accompanied by eye contact and a relaxed mouth and forehead. Ensure your head is up and you're not staring at the ground.

Are you anxious and angry, or relaxed, open, and smiling? If the suggestion you are trying to turn down isn't offensive, then you can add a smile, shake your head, and say, "No, thank you." This is enough to get the job done.

> Pay attention to your voice. Your tone and volume are powerful communicators and modifiers of your words. Are you trying to come across as considerate, gentle, kind, and caring? Is your voice high-pitched? Is it squeaky or nervous? Are you afraid to speak? Does your voice crack when you try to communicate? Do you mumble, or are you loud? Are you bold and blunt? What emotions are you trying to project? Is there a chance you're giving an impression you don't mean to give?

If you'd like to know how your voice sounds to understand the impact of your communication, start by asking people who know you well. Ask them to be honest with you. Remember, through your tone of voice, you can communicate kindness, warmth, dominance, love, insecurity, and confidence, as well as a host of other characteristics.

Also, try to find some positive words to accompany your "No." You don't want to offend the other person. Even though "No" itself is and should be enough, you may want to add some kind words to lighten the impact. Consider phrases like: *"That's nice, but no," "I hope you'll ask me again, but no, I can't make it this weekend,"* or *"No, drinking isn't my thing, but I'd love to study together, go to the movies, or just hang out sometime."*

Ultimately, the goal is to tie together your words, body language, facial expressions, and voice.

Creating Boundaries and Managing Conflicts

Boundaries are critical to any healthy relationship and help foster emotional well-being. The skills emphasized in DBT provide an excellent foundation for creating and maintaining healthy boundaries and navigating relationships better.

First, let's recognize the role of mindfulness, self-validation, and interpersonal effectiveness in creating healthy boundaries.

You may be wondering, "But how can mindfulness help create healthy boundaries?"

Well, it forces you to focus on the present moment so you can recognize your thoughts, feelings, and needs. You can better understand your emotional triggers, recognize positive and negative patterns in your relationships, and gain insight into the kind of boundaries you should create and maintain. This thoughtful awareness empowers you with the knowledge and skills to set limits that protect your mental health, therefore promoting healthy and balanced relationships.

Mindfulness allows you to engage in self-reflection and self-compassion so you can recognize your needs and prioritize your well-being. This is the kind of self-awareness that leads to assertive and effective communication and boundary-setting.

Interpersonal effectiveness teaches us how to communicate assertively and resolve conflicts easily. By practicing effective strategies for managing conflicts and negotiating compromises, you'll know when your boundaries are being crossed and what you can do about it.

How to Set Boundaries

The following are practical ways to start setting boundaries:

- **Be self-aware.**
Self-awareness plays a big part in all our relationships. To set boundaries, begin by developing a better understanding of your viewpoint. Why do you think the way you do? Why do you feel a certain way? What is it about the issue that's making you angry and causing conflict? It's best to understand yourself first before approaching a conflict. Once you understand yourself, it's easier to have meaningful conversations.

- **Self-reflect.**
Once you are self-aware, it's time to move on to self-reflection. Reflect on your boundaries and expectations so you can clearly communicate them. Ask yourself important questions: *What are my values? What are my goals and responsibilities in this relationship? What part have I played in this situation?* Think about your needs and wants. What are the consequences of compromising your values? What's the price of violating your boundaries? How do you feel when your values are respected? How do you feel when they are violated?

- **Make your boundaries and expectations clear to others.**
No one will know your boundaries if you don't communicate them. Speak clearly and be direct. Be specific about what you are and are not willing to put up with. Use the tips discussed earlier to improve your communication. Be assertive yet kind and respectful. Your tone of voice and body language should be respectful, too. Stay consistent in following through with boundaries but maintain some flexibility. Be open to suggestions and feedback because that's how you can learn and grow. When situations change, adjust your boundaries.

- **Don't tell people what they should do.**
You don't need to boss people around. Instead, tell them what you will do. Remember that you are only in control of your own actions; you can't control what other people do. Think ahead, predict any resistance, and find ways to incorporate that into your plan.

Even after doing all this, some people may not respect your boundaries or agree with you. They may have conflicting boundaries of their own. This can lead to resistance, which makes the relationship more challenging. How do you deal with this response? By listening actively.

Listen carefully to the other person and show them you're paying attention. Think about their point of view and try to understand where they're coming from. Incorporate verbal and non-verbal cues—nod, ask questions, mirror them in body language, and paraphrase what they just said.

Be empathic. Validate the other person's feelings. Try to put yourself in their shoes and acknowledge what they feel and the needs they are communicating. You may not agree with them, but when you validate their concerns, they'll feel respected and heard.

Creating boundaries and communicating them is an ongoing process. It's like a fence requiring regular monitoring and maintenance, particularly when a style changes or evolves. To do this the right way, check in with yourself and the other person occasionally. Talk about your boundaries and expectations and analyze their current relevance. Are they still realistic? Are they still reasonable? If there's a need for adjustment, communicate it clearly and respectfully. Reinforce your boundaries again and praise and appreciate the person who respects and meets them. Also, take the opportunity to provide constructive feedback to those who don't respect your boundaries. Speak to them about the importance of mutual trust and respect.

If you have a hard time setting, speaking, and sticking to your boundaries, or if others constantly violate or disrespect them, talk to someone experienced, like your parents or another adult. They can give you advice and encouragement where you need it and serve as mediators.

Conflict Resolution Using DBT Principles

Conflict resolution is a critical part of interpersonal effectiveness, which can be significantly improved using DBT principles. But how?

You already know that DBT is based on the idea of finding a balance between accepting ourselves as we are and finding ways to change the negatives, which can be very helpful when dealing with interpersonal conflicts. When you learn to recognize and validate the emotions of everyone involved in a situation, you can use DBT skills to find a more compassionate and empathetic approach to resolving conflicts. By focusing on acceptance, you can minimize defensiveness and encourage open communication, which leads to more productive discussions and solutions.

> DBT encourages change and growth in interpersonal relationships. Through DBT skills, you learn to take responsibility for your actions and work on improving your communication skills and problem-solving strategies. You'll learn to resolve conflicts healthily and constructively.
>
> Remember, DBT builds mindfulness and non-judgmental awareness, which is critical in conflict resolution. By being present in the moment and fully engaged in the conflict resolution process, you will understand your emotions better, manage your reactions, and respect other people's perspectives, which leads to better conflict resolution.

Sometimes, conversations turn into arguments when you become defensive and respond to criticisms, unpleasant body language, and negative tones of voice. Maybe your sibling started criticizing you about something they don't like about you. Maybe their tone of voice was hostile or defensive.

Now, you're responding to their attacks and insults instead of focusing on their complaint. Staying focused on the goal can be hard. You may have to ignore their attacks. This is actually a DBT skill called ignoring attacks. Instead of responding in a similar hostile way, ignoring attacks encourages the other person to start behaving reasonably so you can revisit the main point.

People often criticize and attack others because it helps them blow off steam, divert the direction of the conversation to something else, or because they enjoy eliciting a reaction. But when you learn to ignore criticism and rise above it, it no longer has power over you. The power others' behavior has over you stops working, and when that happens, they stop the problematic behavior. Of course, there are certain things you must not ignore. Don't overlook emotionally or physically abusive behavior, physical threats, or any indication that you are in danger.

Several DBT skills will come in handy during conflict resolution. But you will need everything you've learned in interpersonal effectiveness, which revolves around setting boundaries, negotiation skills, and assertiveness. This is how you can communicate your needs and boundaries effectively, clearly, and respectfully, which is critical in rationally resolving conflicts.

Interpersonal Effectiveness Exercises

Stepping up your interpersonal effectiveness boosts your abilities in a game where the major skills needed are communication, understanding, and empathy. Here are some exercises to help you develop these skills.

1. The DEAR MAN Technique

This is a handy technique for tough conversations that need clarity and assertiveness. It's a bit complex because the communication must not in any way alter the relationship with the other person. It helps you ensure that your needs and feelings are well expressed while you still respect other perspectives.

D - Describe: Begin by describing what has happened and be clear and factual. Don't allow emotions to control your words.

E - Express: How does this description make you feel? Use the 'I' statements so you're not blaming the other person.

A - Assert: State your thoughts directly and assertively but avoid aggression.

R - Reinforce: After asserting your needs, reinforce them with reasons why they are beneficial. Explain all this to the other person and give them a chance to reason with you.

M - Mindful: Make sure you're being mindful while conversing. If the focus begins to shift, bring it back and stay on track. Avoid distractions or emotional moments.

A - Appear Confident: Make sure everything about your physical appearance, e.g. your body language, tone, and diction, indicates confidence. Keep eye contact, be calm, and state your needs clearly and respectfully.

N - Negotiate: There's always room for common ground. Be ready to give and take. If there is a need, compromise and find a solution that favors both parties. Negotiation is all about settling with what's convenient and best for both parties.

2. The GIVE Technique

This technique complements the DEAR MAN technique and focuses more on the manner of message delivery and interaction with others.

G - Gentle:
This is important because as humans, we tend to react to emotional outbursts. Being gentle helps you avoid attacks, threats, or even judgments. Even when you are angry, you still have to be calm and respectful. Make every effort to communicate and be gentle!

I - Interested:
Show genuine concern for the other person's perspective. Don't just hear what they are saying, but actively listen without judging or interrupting. Maintain eye contact, be attentive, and show that you're fully engaged in the conversation.

V - Validate:
This entails acknowledgment and acceptance. Even when you don't agree with someone's perspectives or opinions, don't invalidate them.

E - Easy Manner:
Your aura during a conversation could mean a lot and influence the interpretation the other person has of you. Communicate in a relaxed and non-threatening manner, ensuring your voice is calm, and that you're speaking with a friendly tone. This keeps the atmosphere positive and open.

3. Mutual Validation

Communication can be difficult when the other person feels like their feelings are being ignored. That's why mutual validation is important. Make sure the other person feels seen and heard and that their thoughts and feelings are being validated. Try to communicate your point of view while doing this at the same time. This doesn't mean you should agree with someone blindly, but simply that you try to understand them.

Here's how it can go: You might say, "I understand you think or feel this way. For my part, I think/feel…"

Think of a difficult relationship you have right now, one where you often have a hard time communicating. Try to explain your point of view using the skill of mutual validation.

Step 1: Try to validate the other person's point of view.

- Situation:

- "I understand that ………………………………………………………………………
………………………………………………………………………………………………
……………………………………………………………………………………………"

- "For my part, ……………………………………………………………………………
………………………………………………………………………………………………
……………………………………………………………………………………………"

Step 2: Use a phrase that explains your request.

- Situation:

- "I think we should be united in ....
....
...."

- "For my part, ...
....
...."

Step 3: Repeat your point of view.

- Situation:

- "What exactly is bothering you about this situation? I think ....
....
...."

As we conclude this chapter, keep in mind that social interaction is a skill that needs continual improvement. Nobody masters the piano on the first day of learning, and it's the same for social interactions. It requires practice, patience, and a genuine willingness to improve.

Chapter 6
Coping with Stressors

We all experience stress in different phases of our lives, and it's important we learn how to manage it. Keep in mind that managing stressors doesn't mean you will have a stress-free life, but learning effective stress management strategies will provide you with opportunities to work through stressful times.

The American Psychological Association reports that teens are usually more stressed than adults (Bethune, S., 2014). Data from this research indicates that most teens know that stress isn't healthy, but many of them underestimate the impact it has on their physical and mental health.

Let's meet Tony, who recently realized that he doesn't cope well with stress. Lately, he's had certain experiences that opened his eyes and made him think about learning better ways to cope with stressors. Both at school and home, Tony has been taking out his stress on others. He's been getting into more arguments with his friends, so many have turned away from him, no longer inviting him over like they used to. Now, he feels bad, helpless, and out of control.

He is desperate to mend his relationships, but he's having a hard time expressing his feelings. He doesn't know how to speak about his thoughts and needs. He doesn't know why he keeps lashing out at people who have done nothing wrong to him. He genuinely doesn't understand why he can't get his actions and emotions under control.

Tony notices a huge difference in how stress affects him and how the people around him cope with it. He can't wrap his head around how easily others manage their stress. They seem calm and less affected by pressure, while he is easily wound up. When he sits back and thinks about his reactions, he admits that sometimes his actions aren't proportional to the problems he experiences. Unfortunately, he can't see it until after the problem has passed.

After thinking about his desire to cope with stressors better, Tony admits that counseling might be a good thing to try. After a few sessions, the therapist introduces a DBT approach. Tony starts to learn about new and effective ways to cope with his stressors. Now, he is learning to express his needs better at school and home. He feels much happier than he was feeling before.

Just like Tony, this chapter will help you cope with a world of stressors. First, let's discuss understanding your triggers.

Understanding Your Stress Triggers

Stress comes when you least expect it. It has patterns and triggers, and below are some possible triggers.

- **Academic**

  One of the most common sources of stress in teens is school. Up to 83% of teens admit that they are often stressed about school — 69% are worried about getting into good colleges, deciding what they want to do after graduation, and the financial impact of those decisions on their families (Ortega, S. 2023).

  Many teens admit to losing sleep, overeating, eating unhealthy foods, or even skipping meals due to stress. They feel angry, irritable, and anxious, and others report feeling tired, overwhelmed, and exhausted.

  In the study, 26% of teens admitted that they snapped at a friend or family member due to stress. About half said they'd been told by someone that they seemed stressed. During the school year, teens have an astonishing 5.8–10 stress level compared to 4.6 during the summer.

  A large percentage of teens worry about their grades, impressing teachers, and keeping up academically with their peers. If they have poor management and coping skills, they may feel overwhelmed by the ever-mounting academic stressors.

- **Social**

  Teens place a great deal of value on their social lives and spend much of their waking hours with or trying to keep up with their friends on social media. They need to find a place where they belong and can keep their social circles intact. This desire can often cause stress. Bullying and more subtle relationship frictions can lead to significant stress for a teen. And as we've learned, managing relationships and coping with stress isn't an easy task for a developing brain.

  Peer pressure and the need to fit in can also lead to stress. In their desire to build and maintain their social circles, teenagers often find themselves taking part in behaviors they would otherwise not engage in just to fit in with or appease their friends.

- **Family Discord**

Stress is often felt by all family members. Anything impacting the family impacts the children, as well. These stressors can come in the form of unrealistic expectations from family members, marital issues between parents, strained sibling relationships, sibling bullying or rivalry, sickness or death in the family, or financial stress.

- **World Events**

Economic downturns, natural disasters, school shootings, and terrorism are scary world events that worry teens as much as they do parents. Teens often talk about these things in private. The bits of scary news at home and abroad can leave them wondering how safe they or their loved ones are.

- **Traumatic Events**

Loss of a family member or friend, long-term illness of a loved one, accidents, physical or emotional abuse, and other traumatic events can all lead to heightened stress levels in teens.

- **Significant Life Changes**

Significant life changes affect teens just as they do adults. Moving to a new neighborhood or changes in the family setup as a result of divorce or blending families can cause tremendous stress for a growing brain. Not knowing how to cope with such stressors can lead to a buildup of stress, which can be overwhelming and confusing.

Stress overload can lead to anxiety, withdrawal from things we love, physical illness, drug and alcohol abuse, or suicidal thoughts, among other detrimental things.

Other potential causes of stress for teens include:
- Living in unsafe surroundings.
- Pressure to be sexually active.
- Housing issues, such as homelessness or being a foster child.
- Negative thought patterns about themselves.
- Getting into college.
- Body changes.
- Uncertainty about the future.
- Mental health issues like anxiety and depression.

When stressed, teens can also show:

- **Emotional changes:**

You may become angry, agitated, anxious, or suffer from mental health issues like depression or anxiety. Pay attention to your behavior.

- **Physical changes:**

We are more likely to become sick when stressed. You may experience headaches, stomach aches, or other pains.

- **Behavioral changes:**

When stressed, you may notice a shift in sleeping and eating habits. You may sleep or eat too little or too much. When you find yourself avoiding things you loved doing in the past, you may be stressed.

- **Cognitive changes:**

You may notice a decrease in concentration. For example, you become more forgetful or your mind wanders.

Organizing Your Life to Minimize Stress

The demands of school, social life, family, and personal interests can pile up, leaving you feeling like you're juggling ten balls at once. Here, we'll explore the invaluable skills of time management to help you organize your time effectively, reduce the feeling of being overwhelmed, and restore balance to your daily routine.

- **Put Your Priorities in Order**
  One of the first steps to effective time management is to understand that tasks carry different levels of importance. To prioritize your tasks, think about the importance each one carries and arrange them accordingly. The Eisenhower Matrix is a tool that can help you categorize your tasks in order of importance. Ensure the things topping your priority list are things that make your life better, and do them before attending to the less important tasks. This will help you reduce stress and organize your life.

- **Set SMART Goals**
  Setting goals gives you a map that can guide you to achieve whatever you want. Setting **SMART** goals helps you actualize your dreams. **SMART** stands for:

  Specific: Make your goals clear and avoid ambiguity. For example, 'I want to be a better keyboardist' is different from 'I want to learn to play on keys A and E.' See the specificity? That's what it means to be specific with your goals.

  Measurable: Set goals you can track and measure when you've made progress. For instance, you can set a goal for yourself to do twenty push-ups daily. Once you hit twenty, you know you've achieved the goal for the day.

  Achievable: Set goals that are feasible and realistic. Look at the long-term possibilities before you set any goal. You can't aim to become a medical doctor in a year. That's impossible; be realistic.

  Relevant: Set goals that are relevant to your existence and growth. For example, if you're passionate about singing, set a goal to improve your vocal range.

  Time-Bound: Set a deadline for your goal. Don't leave it open or you may never achieve it. Set a timeframe and work toward it. This will give you some sense of urgency.

  SMART goals keep you motivated and closer to actualizing your dreams. Try utilizing them and watch your dreams gradually become realities.

- **The Art of Planning**
  Where do you want to go? What's your goal? How do you plan to achieve it? How long will it take you? These are questions that a good planner has answers to. In every plan, clarity is essential. Big dreams may seem impossible, but have you tried breaking them down into smaller and more achievable bits? All journeys, no matter how long, begin with a step.

  Make sure everything doesn't happen at the same time. Prioritize based on importance and create a schedule to complete things. You may encounter disruptions occasionally, but that's normal. Take care to make your plans flexible so they can be tweaked when unexpected circumstances arise.

  Celebrate your small wins, and don't let mistakes dampen your spirit. Mistakes are a stepping stone, and we learn from them. Whatever you want to achieve, plan it properly, and you'll be a few steps closer to your goals.

- **Delegate and Learn to Say No**
  Some people try to do everything on their own, but delegation eases the work burden and boosts effectiveness. This is especially relevant in cases of group work. Split the work and make the task ahead easier for others and yourself.

  If saying yes to certain tasks contradicts your wishes, it's okay to decline. This is an indirect form of self-care because when you're overworked, you are more likely to break down.

  Work on discovering your strengths and focus more energy on them. Always offer to take care of areas where you are strong and trust your other group members to do their part well. If you have ideas, speak up and discuss them with your team.

  Once you understand delegation and how to decline certain things, you'll have more time for yourself and reduce your stress.

- **Rest Your Way to Less Stress**
  When you're stressed, the best thing to do is to rest. Just like how our smartphone needs to be charged when the battery is low, rest recharges us and allows us to think more clearly. Choose quality over quantity, though, because a short nap well taken is better than a long sleep filled with disturbances. Stay away from your gadgets and create a conducive sleep atmosphere for yourself. Good rest boosts productivity, and once you embrace it, you'll become more resilient in the face of stress.

Exercises to Cope with Stressors

The following exercises will help you cope with stressors.

1. Improving the Moment

Here are some ways you can make the current moment better when you're feeling stressed:

- Visualize a calm setting. Imagine a white sandy beach, a beautiful cloudless sky, or someplace in nature. Anything that makes you happy.
- Ask someone for help.
- Unplug all your devices. Try doing nothing and give yourself a "mental vacation."
- Encourage yourself by repeating positive phrases like, *"I can do this," "I can manage this," "This is something I can stand,"* and *"I have the power to stay calm."* Be your own cheerleader and hype yourself up.

2. Imaginary Bubble

This is a form of controlled breathing that can help distract you from whatever upsets you.

- Hold your hands in front of your face. Your palms should be together as if you're praying.
- Create an imaginary bubble with your hands.
- Now, blow into the imaginary bubble.
- Move your hands slightly to create more space for the bubble every time you blow into it.
- Your imaginary bubble should grow bigger with each blow.
- The slower and deeper you blow, the bigger your imaginary bubble grows. If your breaths are small and fast, the bubble still grows, but not as much as with slow breaths.
- Blow into the bubble and grow it until you calm down. Once you're calm, pop the bubble and blow it away.

3. Self-Massage

Sit in a comfortable position and knead the muscles around your neck and shoulders. Create a loose fist, then drum swiftly up and down the back of your neck and its sides. Next, work tiny circles around the base of your skull using your thumbs. Then, massage your scalp with your fingertips. Make small taps against your scalp with your fingers, slowly moving from the front to the back and then to the sides.

Move on to your face. Create tiny circles with your fingertips and thumbs. Pay more attention to the muscles along your jaw, forehead, and temples. Using your middle finger, massage the bridge of your nose. Slowly work outward to your eyebrows and then temples.

4. Journaling

Journaling is like creating a space where you can rant and freely express yourself without judgment. You're free to do and undo, and this is done by documenting moments, both positive and negative. Journaling also aids your self-discovery, because you will probably find out things you never knew about yourself. There's no standard way to go about journaling, so do it in any way that pleases you. You might very well even derive joy from doing it, especially as time passes. Journaling is a perfect self-expression tool, so embrace it and reap its benefits.

If you use any of the techniques we've discussed, you'll become more resilient, understanding, and more easily be able to manage the stress of life. Remember to view stressors as opportunities for growth rather than as negative experiences.

Chapter 7
Social Media and Mental Health

You pick up your phone and open your Instagram app. Some awesome content catches your attention and you're smiling. But before you know it, you're scrolling through posts that make you feel like everyone's life is perfect except yours. You decide to close the app and do something else. If this has happened to you, you're not alone.

Too many people, both teens and adults, compare their lives with the highlights they see on social media. One cleverly-edited picture is used to represent an individual's entire life. But we should all know by now that these beautiful pictures and captions are not reality. Their impact on how you feel about yourself cannot be underrated.

This chapter will discuss the relationship between social media and your mental well-being. We'll discuss the positives and negatives, and how you can navigate the space with your mental health in check. Let's get started.

Benefits of Social Media

No matter what people may think about the technological innovation known as social media, it does have its bright sides. It's a tool one can use to achieve many things, even beyond the imagination. Some of these benefits are:

- **Enhanced Communication**
  One significant benefit of social media is that it has made communication incredibly easy. It's a like a bridge between you and the world. With a gadget as small as your mobile phone, you can quickly connect with anyone anywhere. As a teenager, you can use social media to connect with people who have the same interests as you and learn about people from different cultures and backgrounds. Facebook and similar platforms allow you to collaborate outside of class and share ideas about assignments. Some schools even use blog sites as teaching tools, which can enhance writing.

- **Creativity and Entertainment**
  Social media has opened new possibilities for entertainment and sharing. With access to a range of creative tools, you can explore your interests and express yourself in new and exciting ways. It also makes it possible to promote causes that you believe in, raise money for charity, and volunteer for political and charitable events. So, no matter what you are into, social media is an important tool to hone and display your craft. Take care to use it positively and remember to strike a balance with your real life so it doesn't become detrimental.

- **Learning about Technology**
  The media space goes beyond endless scrolling. It is a place where you can gain knowledge that can set you on the path to success. Social media has become part of our everyday lives, and through its use, we can acquire technical skills that make the transition from high school to college easier. Also, learning how to express yourself online prepares you for future opportunities in the workplace.

- **Removes Boundaries**
  Social media is an endless bridge that can hold as many people as necessary. It brings people closer, without the limitations of physical factors. It has turned the world into a global community. It enhances bonds and allows us to connect with people beyond borders. It helps those with disabilities connect with others and build a support system so they can spend time with their peers. And being able to talk to people online allows us to strengthen relationships with our loved ones and communicate with those we don't see every day.

- **Career Opportunities**
  Social media is an excellent place to get your career started. It's a valid door opener to many opportunities you can key into, and it keeps creating more and more career opportunities. With the rise of the digital economy, there is a growing demand for workers with digital skills and expertise. Learning how to effectively use digital tools and platforms can prepare you for the job market and future success.

Drawbacks of Social Media for Teens

Despite the benefits of social media, it also has a dark side. The effects of social media are generally detrimental to the mental health of teenagers. Let's go over some of the reasons.

- **Molding Aspirations**

  Social media is like a coin, with advantages on one side and disadvantages on the other. It can inspire and connect us to possibilities, but it is also capable of causing us to put unnecessary pressure on ourselves, and this affects how we perceive reality.

  The more you use social media, the more you feel compelled to align with certain trends for validation, and become a victim of peer pressure. This can lead you to nurture unrealistic expectations of how you should live your life, because you live by what you see rather than what you believe to be right.

  Comparison is one of the biggest problems social media breeds. At some point, you may feel like you're not doing enough because you're using another person's posts as a yardstick for your own successes. It's important to understand that what you see in someone else's posts is rarely reality, and that you need to live your own life.

  When it comes to a career, take care to consume content that will help yours in a positive way. Often the lifestyle social media influencers post about can make us feel like we're not doing well in our career, and we start doubting ourselves and wondering if we should switch careers to whatever the influencer does for a living. This can lead you down the wrong path. Follow your passion and interests and ignore what you see, because it is almost certainly not reality.

  When we're overexposed to certain lifestyles, we tend to want to replicate what people are doing on social media instead of mining our own creativity and finding something fantastic. Not everything that trends is positive. Sleep deprivation even goes beyond the physical effects. It can trigger conditions like ADHD, anxiety, and even depression. Ensure you strike a balance between your online presence and getting the required sleep your body needs.

- **Sleep Deprivation**

    When you spend so much time scrolling through various social media platforms, you'll never reach the end, and this affects your sleep patterns. No matter how long you spend scrolling, there will always be more. This disruption of your sleep pattern can quickly develop into bigger problems. Your mood is affected when you're deprived of quality sleep. You feel irritable, making it difficult to face the problems of life with an optimistic attitude. Your academic performance suffers because sleep is basic to your cognitive functioning and memory consolidation.

    Sleep deprivation even goes beyond the physical effects. It can trigger conditions like ADHD, anxiety, and even depression. Ensure you strike a balance between your online presence and getting the required sleep your body needs.

- **Conformity**

    As a teen, there's a natural urge to want to belong, and social media plays a huge role in exploiting this. It's where you come across a lot of norms and behaviors, and the pressure can make you adopt these behaviors and habits, either consciously or unconsciously. You try to fit into a mold determined by strangers on social media even when it doesn't fit who you are.

    When you find yourself trying to dress, speak, or act like certain influencers or celebrities, even when the behaviors don't align with your true identity, you're trying to conform. As you grow, you should be able to recognize when conformity sets in and be able to deal with it. Your identity is your most valuable asset!

- **Fear of Missing Out (FOMO)**

    FOMO is becoming increasingly prevalent with the rise of social media, and it is extremely potent in teenagers, since teens are at a stage in life where peer acceptance is crucial. Chances are, you feel compelled to stay online for a long time so you don't miss out on anything, and you're probably driven to check social media constantly to see what others are doing. FOMO can make you less creative, affect your sleep patterns, and trigger feelings like anxiety. Feeling the need to stay updated so you know what others are doing can be stressful mentally. Work toward balancing how you stay connected and taking some time off to look after your mental health.

- **Cyberbullying**

    This is a significant and insidious issue on social media. There are millions of hurtful comments, mean messages, and even threats out there, a large percentage of which are targeted at teens. These can cause problems and may even skyrocket to worse issues like anxiety, low self-esteem, sadness, depression, and isolation.

    The consequences of this terrible behavior go beyond the mental sphere but also affect victims physically and in their overall well-being. It's important to learn how to protect yourself online and where to seek help if you experience cyberbullying.

    Balancing your online and offline lives is vital to your health. Social media is an amazing innovation for connections and self-expression, but there are plenty of dangers. Make sure you're using it positively and prioritizing your well-being.

Digital Detox

Digital detox is becoming more and more popular, as people try to escape the fast-paced and always-on digital world and rediscover the importance of a balanced life. Whether the goal is to reduce stress, focus on academics, improve sleep, or simply take a break from technology, digital detox can help.

Digital detox means staying away from all your devices, including your phone, tablet, and laptop, and limiting technology use so you can reconnect with real life and enhance your well-being. It's important to understand that as much as social media can be a source of educational information, it can also be harmful to your mental health. Endless stimulation and distraction are exhausting and stressful to the brain, especially a developing one. Detox allows your brain to recharge and provides space for deeper thinking, improves moods, and reduces anxiety and depression. Unplugging helps to relieve the pressure of FOMO and lets you appreciate real life and emotions.

The detox period can be any amount of time, but it's important to adhere to whatever timeframe you choose.

Benefits of a Digital Detox

Mental Clarity: Spending too much time on social media can clog up your mental space. If you take a break from the constant flow of information, you'll allow your mind to have some peace. This can help you be more creative and self-reflective, and as a result, your thoughts will be clearer and you'll be better able to focus on things that truly matters.

Reduced Stress: Those who are constantly on social media have phone notifications that are always active. They feel pressure to stay updated, and this contributes to high stress levels. Living a life of comparison with others can cause great stress. A digital detox gives you a break from all that peer pressure, which can reduce your stress.

Improved Sleep: Being glued to gadgets can seriously affect your sleep, especially at bedtime. The human body has something called a circadian rhythm, and this rhythm is disrupted by the blue light that eminates from screens, so getting a good night's sleep becomes difficult. A digital detox will help you disconnect from your screens, and your body will enjoy good quality sleep and return to a normal cycle. When you wake up, you'll feel refreshed and ready for the day's activities.

Enhanced Productivity: We all have our productive times, but if we don't manage our time, social media will eat into it. Digital detox forces you to manage your media engagement, and you'll be able to focus and concentrate with no distractions. Create a conducive workspace and keep your gadgets out of it. You'll be indirectly boosting your productivity, and you'll get more done in a shorter amount of time.

Reconnect with Real Life: What you see on social media is seldom reality. The truth is, it can make you delusional about many things, but Digital detox pushes you out of that virtual cage and compels you to engage with the physical world. You'll connect with nature, family, and friends and enjoy natural activities that give you joy. This can do you a world of good, and the bonus is that you might appreciate nature more than you ever did before.

Mindful Consumption: Evaluating your digital behaviors and the content you consume is very important. You should be intentional and know why you use social media. This awareness will help you make good decisions about how you use it. Try to be selective about the content you engage with and make sure it aligns with your interests and values.

Planning your Digital Detox

Set Boundaries:
Define your boundaries for your detox and state the duration. Write down how long you want it to last, whether it's a few hours, a day, weeks, or even longer. Then decide which devices and platforms you want to disconnect from.

Designate Disconnection Periods:
Detox is about detachment, so you need to be specific about the periods when you'll be offline. Make sure your friends and family are aware of these times, too, so nobody will complain that you've been unavailable.

Find Alternative Activities:
One of the best ways to get rid of something is to replace it. To make your digital detox fun and fulfilling, find activities you can engage with during the time you're offline. When you have replacements, there is less temptation to return to social media.

Digital detox is a personal decision, and there's no manual for it. The main goal is to try to strike a balance between your online and offline worlds, so do it in a way that works for you.

Digital Detox Exercises

A digital detox is like flushing out your system.

Below are some exercises and worksheets that can help your process.

1. Is Social Media a Problem?

Use this worksheet to determine whether your social media use is becoming an issue. Write true or false next to each statement.

- Others have told me that I'm on social media way too much.
- I've put off my responsibilities because I was too focused on my phone.
- I've tried to cut back on my social media use, but I can't do it.
- I refresh my social media feeds multiple times in one sitting.
- It is hard for me to go a few minutes without checking my phone.
- Having my phone taken away from me is devastating.
- I've kept myself from falling asleep so I could stay on my phone.
- I feel like I'm missing out on something if I do not check my phone regularly.
- I've lied to a teacher, parent, or adult about being on my phone.
- I'd rather interact with others on social media than face to face.
- Being on my phone is the only thing that makes me happy.
- Checking my phone is the first thing I do when I wake up.
- Being on social media has a strong influence on my mood, attitude, and behavior.

2. Digital Detox Planner

This planner is a guide to embark on your detox journey. It will help you to structure, plan, and achieve your digital detox. Feel free to tweak to your taste.

Step 1: Define the Duration

Look at your routine and come up with a good duration for your digital detox. A weekend? A few days? A whole month? Be specific about the timeframe.

Step 2: Setting Clear Boundaries

Write out the boundaries for this effort and describe them in detail.

> Write out the days and times you'll be offline. For example, you may decide to stay off social media from 10 a.m. to 6 p.m. every day.

What gadgets will you avoid? Be specific and write them out.

Are there any exceptions for these rules to be broken? Write them down.

Are there any exceptions for these rules to be broken? Write them down.

Step 3: Plan Alternative Activities

Digital detox isn't just about detaching from social media but also exploring a world beyond the online space. Use this section of the worksheet to come up with alternative activities.

What are your hobbies or interests you wish to pursue?

What outdoor activities do you enjoy? For example, cycling, hiking, etc.

Make a list of books from various genres you've been eager to read.

What activities can you engage in with loved ones to strengthen your bonds?

Step 4: Reflect and Journal

Ensure you properly document your journey during your digital detox in this section.

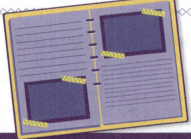

Jot down how you feel, your challenges, and highlights on a daily basis. How did this detox affect your daily life and emotions?

Write down any new hobbies or interests you tried during your detox. How did these make you feel?

What changes did you notice about your mental well-being? Did you experience less stress or greater clarity?

What are you grateful for during your digital detox?

Step 5: Post-Detox Reflection

After concluding your detox, set aside some time to reflect on the experience.

Give a summary of the highlights and lessons you learned.

Describe the difficulties you faced and how you were able to manage them.

How will you infuse the lessons you've learned into your daily routine, and what changes will you make?

This detox planner is only a guide to help you through your detox. Feel free to customize it to suit your needs. Best of luck as you embark on the road to reconnecting with yourself and the world around you!

3. Social Media Questionnaire

The main social media platforms I use are:

...., ...,

...., ...

I like these more than the others because ....

....

....

I'm on these platforms for at least .... hours a day.

How does using social media affect my mood, attitude, or behavior?

....

....

....

....

....

....

Write yes or no beside each statement below.

- I feel left out or excluded sometimes when using social media.
- I hide parts of who I am when using social media.
- I feel anxious when I make a post on social media. Why? ....
  ....
  ....

- Social media sometimes makes me feel worse about myself.
- I've engaged in bullying and trolling on social media.
- I feel bad when no one comments on or likes what I post.
- I feel like I can be myself when I'm on social media.
- Some adults in my life have an issue with my social media use.
- I've had people make negative comments or bully me on social media.
- Social media makes me feel more popular.
- Social media makes me feel less lonely.
- I've said things I've regretted on social media.
- Social media makes me feel better about myself.

Use the exercises and worksheets in this chapter to plan, track, and reflect on your digital detox journey.

Chapter 8
Self-Care and Self-Compassion

When we become caught up in the hustle and bustle of school, work, relationships, and social media, we often forget to take care of ourselves, but we're the most important person in our life, so it's vital to engage in regular self-care.

In spite of what its perception is in the media, self-care does not mean treating yourself to a luxurious lifestyle; it is a necessity to maintain good health. In this chapter, you'll get back in touch with your very first best friend: you! You'll embrace compassion and learn how self-care can benefit your life and the lives of those around you.

Remember, the greatest asset you have is you!

Understanding Self-Care and Self-Compassion

Self-care refers to caring for your physical, mental, and emotional well-being. Don't listen to those who think it's selfish of you to focus on yourself. Self-care shows you know your worth and that you treat yourself with kindness and respect.

Self-care covers many different things, but they all work together to revive your mind, body, and spirit. It's also about knowing when you need a break or when you need to engage in certain activities to feel happy.

Self-compassion, on the other hand, is like thinking of yourself as your best friend and doing things for yourself that you would do for them. It teaches you to extend all the support, kindness, love, and encouragement that you'd give to your best friend.

Self-compassion encourages you to accept that you're allowed to make mistakes because you're not perfect and reminds you to see this as normal. When tough times come, don't be harsh with yourself. Picture yourself as your best buddy who sees you as worthy of love and forgiveness, regardless of the situation.

The Need for Self-Care and Self-Compassion

Do you know why self-care and self-compassion are crucial for well-being?

Imagine having a friend who sticks with you through thick and thin. Someone who understands, loves, and never judges you. They continually support and push you to do better. Now imagine yourself as that friend. Be your best friend when it matters the most, because you should be your own most enthusiastic supporter.

Let's review the positive sides of these two practices.

Manage Life's Ups and Downs

The teenage years come with so many unavoidable challenges. You need self-care and self-compassion to help make life easier during these times. They are like a safe place to run to during tough times.

Reduce Stress

Many factors will stress you as a teen. Social pressure, exams, deadlines, and even friends will test you, and this can cause anxiety. Self-care allows you to take a break and reduce stress, while self-compassion reminds you to show yourself some kindness and support when you're under pressure.

Boost Resilience

Resilience means you can bounce back after a fall, and this is a very useful trait to possess. Self-care and self-compassion will boost your resilience and teach you to see failure as an opportunity to improve and succeed.

Nurture Mental Health

Be gentle with yourself during hard times, especially when your problems can affect your mental health. Self-compassion allows you to be kind and supportive with yourself, and self-care can take your mind off your troubles.

Foster Healthy Relationships

You can't give what you don't have. When you're kind to yourself, you're more likely to build healthy relationships with those around you. Self-care equips you with the right energy and emotional maturity to connect with others.

Cultivate Self-Understanding

Self-compassion teaches you to reflect on yourself without criticism or judgment, and this leads to self-awareness. When you can reflect on your thoughts and feelings, it helps your personal growth and overall well-being.

Balance Responsibilities

The teenage years come with many responsibilities. As you juggle these, self-care will encourage balance and give you time to relax.

Long-Term Well-being

Self-compassion and self-care will help set a foundation for the long-term and will serve you well for the rest of your life, so take them seriously. They are valuable tools you'll need to face life's challenges, and remind you to be kind to yourself no matter what you're going through.

Nurturing Self-Care

As we've just learned, self-care is a lifelong effort. Let's discuss some aspects of self-care and find out how you can utilize them.

Mental Self-Care

This involves engaging in activities like mindfulness meditation, which helps to stay present and reduce stress, cognitive exercises to challenge the mind, and destressing techniques like deep breathing and journaling. Other activities include finding ways to express your emotions, taking digital detox breaks, seeking support, and practicing self-compassion. All these are vital to your mental health.

Also, positive self-talk and self-reflection make you more aware of yourself and boost your personal growth. Stress management helps keep you sane in the face of stress. Investing in your mental health is one of the best decisions you can make.

Physical Care

This means doing regular exercises, eating a balanced diet, and getting proper hydration to keep your body in good shape. Your sleep routine is equally important. When you sleep well, you're well-charged and ready to face the day ahead. Teens should get 7-9 hours of sleep every day and make an effort to balance their screen time. Basic body hygiene practices like bathing and dental care are also vital.

Don't wait until you have a medical issue to visit your doctor for a checkup and get all necessary vaccinations. Stay away from harmful habits like smoking and substance abuse. Developing all these good habits will pay off when you're an adult.

Emotional Self-Care

Your emotional well-being is just as important as your mental and physical health. Self-compassion, in which you're able to accept your feelings without judgment, and expressing your emotions constructively by talking to a trusted friend or writing in a journal are both included in this effort. Engage in positive activities, as well, and practice gratitude. Consider using a gratitude jar and toss in messages of what you're grateful for every day.

Self-Compassion in Tough Times

When tough times come, self-compassion is needed, but how do you practice it?

- Identify and validate your emotions. It's normal to get angry, sad, or anxious when things don't go as planned. Your feelings are valid, and you should acknowledge them but not react harshly.

- After acknowledging these feelings, have a conversation with yourself, but don't criticize or judge yourself.

- Put yourself in places where you can engage in activities that lift your mood. There's no standard way to do this. Whatever works for you is fine.

- Be mindful of your emotions and stay present. You can do deep breathing to calm yourself.

- Remember to reach out to loved ones for support. No one is an island. If you don't feel like you have supportive friends and family, seek professional support from trained therapists. When you share your feelings, your heart feels lighter.

- Accept yourself as you are. Nobody has everything they need to handle every situation perfectly. Embrace who you are and use your mistakes as stepping stones to learning and growing.

- Don't allow room for negative self-talk. Stay positive and always remind yourself of your potential and capabilities. Affirmations can do a lot for your confidence level.

If life wasn't challenging, we would have no need for self-compassion. But everyone experiences difficulties in life, so don't run away from the hard times. If you do, you won't grow. Extend to yourself the same kindness and love you would give to a close friend, and you'll build your emotional resilience and be able to face whatever life has in store.

Exercises

Below are exercises to help you build a habit of self-compassion and self-care. These tools will help you cope both now as a teenager and as an adult.

1. Positive Affirmations

These are powerful statements that build self-esteem. With positive affirmations, there's no room for negative talk or thoughts. Affirmations that align with you will have greater effect. Write them on a note and post them somewhere you will see them daily. You might also read them aloud to yourself. Incorporating this into your daily routine will put your mindset on the right path, and this will boost your overall well-being.

Some positive affirmations you can use are:

- "I am worthy of love and kindness, especially from myself."
- "I embrace my uniqueness and recognize my strengths."
- "I am resilient, and I can overcome challenges."
- "I trust myself to make decisions that are right for me."
- "I am not defined by my mistakes; they are opportunities for growth."
- "I deserve to take care of my physical and emotional well-being."
- "I am proud of my accomplishments, big or small."
- "I am confident in my abilities and trust in my potential."
- "I am in control of my thoughts, and I choose positivity."
- "I am deserving of success and happiness."
- "I am kind to myself, even when things don't go as planned."
- "I am grateful for the lessons life teaches me."
- "I am capable of creating the life I desire."
- "I am enough just as I am."
- "I am surrounded by love and support from friends and family."

2. Self-Compassion Journal

Use a self-compassion journal as a safe place to pour out your thoughts and feelings without any judgment. Here's a guide on how to get started:

Some positive affirmations you can use are:

- Buy a journal with a cover and format that appeals to you.

- Dedicate time to journaling every day, whether in the morning, afternoon, or before bed. Whatever time of day you choose, try to dedicate a few minutes each time.

- Write about yourself. How do you feel? How's your day going? What are your thoughts and worries, what are you thinking about?

- Be kind to yourself as you write. When experiencing a tough time, write positive and encouraging words of comfort.

- Write positive affirmations you can read aloud to yourself to re-fill your confidence tank.

- Don't wait until you've accomplished something huge before you celebrate. Celebrate the little wins, too. A lot of little ones can make a big one!

- Practice gratitude. Nothing is too unimportant to be grateful for. Make it a habit.

- End every journaling session with a positive message for yourself. For example, *'I am wonderful.'*

Journaling should always be that space where you can rant, embrace who you are, and practice self-compassion.

3. Create a Self-Care Routine

It's a great idea to establish a routine that puts you in the center. Here are some questions to help you craft one.

- What activities make you happy? Write them down.

- What time of day or day of the week will you dedicate to your self-care? Mark it on your calendar and stay faithful to it.

- How much time do you spend glued to your gadgets? Reduce this, take deep breaths, and focus on the present moment.

- What treatments do you give to your body? Get active and try some physically engaging activities. Then take a nice warm bubble bath and relax!

- What is your diet like? Try to consume nutritious foods whenever you can.

- What's your sleep routine like? Do you get between 7 and 9 hours every day? If not, work towards that.

- Stay hydrated. Carry a bottle of water with you when you're out.

- How much time do you spend with your family? Time with loved one can positively affect your mood.

There's no perfect self-care routine. Yours should be unique, just like you are. Don't take your well-being lightly. Take care of yourself. You deserve it.

Remember, practicing self-care and self-compassion isn't a selfish activity. You deserve all the love, kindness, and support that you give to others. Gift yourself a self-care routine, and you won't regret it.

Conclusion

Well done!

Congratulate yourself for staying with me to the end. Now I'd like to share a brief story.

A young woman I know, Christine, had her fair share of life's ups and downs, just like all of you. There were times when everything seemed hopeless, from school pressures and deadlines to friendship headaches to family issues and more. At some point, she became overwhelmed and felt nothing was going to work. Luckily for her, she came across DBT and began exploring its unique capabilities. As she progressed, she began to appreciate what she was learning and started to use the DBT skills, because they help teens cope with life's toughest moments.

Whenever she started to feel overwhelmed by school work, she used **STOP** to catch her breath. When it came to her emotions, she used **RAIN** to stay calm and find inner peace. When she had self-doubt, she journaled and affirmed her worth and relevance.

She discovered that being a teenager wasn't as easy as it seemed but that it was an ideal time for growth and self-discovery. She learned to be kind to herself, embrace her unique nature, and connect with others in deeply meaningful ways.

Sounds awesome, doesn't it? Well, thankfully, the DBT skills, mindfulness practices, and ways to cope with stress that helped Christine are all in this book, and they will help you if you're ready to make the effort.

Remember that with consistency and resilience, your future is bright. Don't forget to celebrate the small wins, because they add up and show you how successful you truly are.

Everyone's story is unique, but none of us is alone. Use DBT skills to enjoy the adventure that is life, and you'll find yourself growing as a human and becoming adept at handling any type of stress, now and forever. **I have faith in you!**

References

1. Emotional Regulation: Skills, Exercises, & Strategies to Regulate. (n.d.). https://www.betterup.com/blog/emotional-regulation-skills

2. Ackerman, C. E., MA. (2023, April 24). 21 Emotion Regulation Worksheets & Strategies. PositivePsychology.com. https://positivepsychology.com/emotion-regulation-worksheets-strategies-dbt-skills/

3. Linehan, M. (n.d.-a). Emotional regulation skills. Dialectical Behavior Therapy (DBT) Tools. https://dbt.tools/emotional_regulation/index.php

4. Linehan, M. (n.d.-b). Opposite action skill. Dialectical Behavior Therapy (DBT) Tools. https://dbt.tools/emotional_regulation/opposite-action.php

5. MSc, O. G. (2023, October 9). Emotional Regulation: Learn Skills To Manage Your Emotions. Simply Psychology. https://www.simplypsychology.org/emotional-regulation.html

6. Daughters, S. B., Gorka, S. M., Rutherford, H. J. V., & Mayes, L. C. (2014). Maternal and adolescent distress tolerance: The moderating role of gender. Emotion, 14(2), 416–424. https://doi.org/10.1037/a0034991

7. Footprints. (2020, September 8). Introduction to Dialectal Behavioural Therapy: The TIPP Skill - Footprints. Footprints - Taking positive steps with you. https://footprintscommunity.org.au/resources/introduction-to-dialectal-behavioural-therapy-the-tipp-skill/#:~:text=One%20of%20our%20favourite%20DBT,are%20going%20to%20consume%20you.

8. MacPherson, H. A., Cheavens, J. S., & Fristad, M. A. (2013). Dialectical behavior therapy for adolescents: theory, treatment adaptations, and empirical outcomes. Clinical child and family psychology review, 16(1), 59–80. https://doi.org/10.1007/s10567-012-0126-7

9. Pederson, L. (2012). The expanded dialectical behavior therapy skills training manual: Practical DBT for self-help, and individual & group treatment settings. Eau Claire, WI: Premier Publishing & Media

10. Ranch, I. Y. (2023, March 23). 5 DBT Skills to Help Your Kids Manage Stress. Youth ranch. https://www.youthranch.org/blog/5-dbt-skills-to-help-your-kids-manage-stress

11. Collegenp. (n.d.). 10 Advantages of Social media for Students | CollegeNP. https://www.collegenp.com/. https://www.collegenp.com/technology/advantages-of-social-media-for-students/

12. Staff, N. A. (2023a, November 9). Effects of social media on teenagers. Newport Academy. https://www.newportacademy.com/resources/well-being/effect-of-social-media-on-teenagers/

13. Rathus, J. H. & Miller, A. L. (2015). DBT skills manual for adolescents. New York, NY: The Guilford Press

14. Staff, N. A. (2023b, November 9). Effects of social media on teenagers. Newport Academy. https://www.newportacademy.com/resources/well-being/effect-of-social-media-on-teenagers/

15. The Annie E. Casey Foundation. (2023, August 10). Social media and teen mental health. https://www.aecf.org/blog/social-medias-concerning-effect-on-teen-mental-health#:~:text=Numerous%20studies%20show%20that%20higher,poor%20body%20image%2C%20eating%20disorder

16. Collegenp. (n.d.). 10 Advantages of Social media for Students | CollegeNP. https://www.collegenp.com/. https://www.collegenp.com/technology/advantages-of-social-media-for-students/

17. Staff, N. A. (2023a, November 9). Effects of social media on teenagers. Newport Academy. https://www.newportacademy.com/resources/well-being/effect-of-social-media-on-teenagers/

18. Staff, N. A. (2023b, November 9). Effects of social media on teenagers. Newport Academy. https://www.newportacademy.com/resources/well-being/effect-of-social-media-on-teenagers/

19. Lawler, M. (2023, August 4). How to do a digital detox. EverydayHealth.com. https://www.everydayhealth.com/emotional-health/how-to-do-a-digital-detox-without-unplugging-completely/

20. Reddy, K. J., Menon, K. R., & Thattil, A. (2017). Understanding Academic Stress among Adolescents. Artha Journal of Social Sciences, 16(1), 39. https://doi.org/10.12724/ajss.40.4

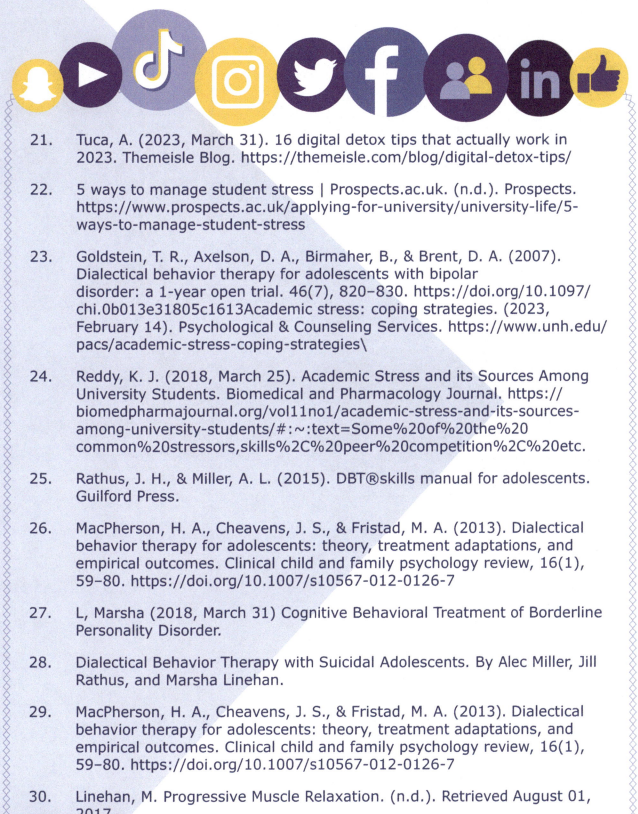

21. Tuca, A. (2023, March 31). 16 digital detox tips that actually work in 2023. Themeisle Blog. https://themeisle.com/blog/digital-detox-tips/

22. 5 ways to manage student stress | Prospects.ac.uk. (n.d.). Prospects. https://www.prospects.ac.uk/applying-for-university/university-life/5-ways-to-manage-student-stress

23. Goldstein, T. R., Axelson, D. A., Birmaher, B., & Brent, D. A. (2007). Dialectical behavior therapy for adolescents with bipolar disorder: a 1-year open trial. 46(7), 820–830. https://doi.org/10.1097/chi.0b013e31805c1613Academic stress: coping strategies. (2023, February 14). Psychological & Counseling Services. https://www.unh.edu/pacs/academic-stress-coping-strategies\

24. Reddy, K. J. (2018, March 25). Academic Stress and its Sources Among University Students. Biomedical and Pharmacology Journal. https://biomedpharmajournal.org/vol11no1/academic-stress-and-its-sources-among-university-students/#:~:text=Some%20of%20the%20common%20stressors,skills%2C%20peer%20competition%2C%20etc.

25. Rathus, J. H., & Miller, A. L. (2015). DBT®skills manual for adolescents. Guilford Press.

26. MacPherson, H. A., Cheavens, J. S., & Fristad, M. A. (2013). Dialectical behavior therapy for adolescents: theory, treatment adaptations, and empirical outcomes. Clinical child and family psychology review, 16(1), 59–80. https://doi.org/10.1007/s10567-012-0126-7

27. L, Marsha (2018, March 31) Cognitive Behavioral Treatment of Borderline Personality Disorder.

28. Dialectical Behavior Therapy with Suicidal Adolescents. By Alec Miller, Jill Rathus, and Marsha Linehan.

29. MacPherson, H. A., Cheavens, J. S., & Fristad, M. A. (2013). Dialectical behavior therapy for adolescents: theory, treatment adaptations, and empirical outcomes. Clinical child and family psychology review, 16(1), 59–80. https://doi.org/10.1007/s10567-012-0126-7

30. Linehan, M. Progressive Muscle Relaxation. (n.d.). Retrieved August 01, 2017

Made in the USA
Las Vegas, NV
30 May 2024

90529999R00057